THE PASSION OF CHRIST

The Passion of Christ

Veselin Kesich

ST VLADIMIR'S SEMINARY PRESS
CRESTWOOD, NEW YORK
2004

Library of Congress Cataloging-in-Publication Data

Kesich, Veselin, 1921–
    The Passion of Christ / Veselin Kesich.—Rev. ed.
        p.   cm.
    Includes bibliographical references.
    ISBN 0–913836–80-x (alk. paper)
    1. Jesus Christ—Passion.   2. Jesus Christ—Biography.   I. Title.
    BT431.3.K47 2004
    232.96—dc22

                                        2004016430

COPYRIGHT © 2004
ST VLADIMIR'S SEMINARY PRESS
575 Scarsdale Rd, Crestwood, NY 10707
1–800–204–2665
www.svspress.com

ISBN 0–913836–80–x

Contents

Introduction

T HIS ESSAY, based on the Gospel account of Christ's passion with some insights from modern scholarship, was written forty years ago. The essential story remains the same. Due to the popular film of this subject[1] and recent studies touching the Crucifixion, there is now widespread interest in the theme.

The passion narrative is the core and heart of Christianity. Whenever Christians debate with non-Christians, the suffering and death on the Cross takes central place. The film, "The Passion of the Christ," provoked various emotions. While some were alarmed by the violence, others were moved by genuine religious experience. The topics dominating scholarly reviews and general discussion are the supposed exaggeration of the importance of the Cross in Christianity and the perceived anti-Semitic tone of the Gospel accounts. Here we shall discuss these two themes.

Crucifixion as extreme punishment was not unknown among the Jews. In the second century BC, after the Maccabee victory over the Hellenistic king Antiochus IV, Pharisees and Sadducees, who emerged from the Maccabee supporters, became

---

[1]"The Passion of the Christ," produced by Mel Gibson and released by Icon Distribution, Inc. 2004.

rivals for the dominant position. The Pharisees, who were against the use of religion for the purpose of political unity, opposed the Maccabees, especially when the Maccabee family claimed not only the throne of Judah, but also the post of High Priest. For their resistance to the ruler, about eight hundred Pharisees were crucified (104–75 BC). When the Pharisees became more influential, they in turn dealt with the Sadducees, the former ruler's advisors, in the same way. With the Roman conquest of Palestine (63 BC), crucifixion became their extreme punishment for political rebellion.

The Romans exerted this power most drastically after the disastrous Jewish-Roman Wars in 70 AD and 135, when Jewish martyrs suffered death by crucifixion. Rabbis sentenced to be crucified at this time expressed fear, not of death, but of being put outside the community of Israel by this punishment. The cross never became an acceptable symbol of Jewish suffering, primarily due to the rabbinical interpretation of the law in Deuteronomy 21.23: "A hanged man is accursed by God" [M. Hengel, *Crucifixion* (Philadelphia: Fortress Press, 1977)].

St Paul deals directly with this law: "Christ redeemed us from the curse of the Law, having become a curse for us—for it is written: 'Cursed be everyone who hangs on the tree'" (Gal 3.12). To the Corinthians he writes: "For our sake God made him to be sin, who knew no sin, so that in him we might become the righteousness of God" (2 Cor 5.21). Jesus stood alongside sinful humanity, and for our sake died on "the tree of shame." For Paul, "He was put to death for our transgressions and raised for our justification" (Rom 4.25). His Cross is a resurrecting cross. His death was that of the suffering Messiah, who accomplished his mission on the Cross. In the Orthodox icon of the Crucifixion, based on John 19.25f, Christ's eyes are closed, as if asleep. His suffering does not distort his face. The viewer expects that he will awaken.

The Cross remains the main divide between Christians and non-Christians. We know Paul's powerful preaching about the Cross: "a *skandalon* to Jews and folly to the Gentiles," but, to both Jews and Gentiles who have been called, "Christ is both the power of God and the Wisdom of God" (1 Cor 1.18f). Christ lived his entire life, not only in his last days, under the shadow of the Cross. The cross on which he was crucified is the most powerful symbol of Christian identity. Its importance cannot be minimized or reduced in the interest of dialogue with other religions.

Some commentators, Christians as well as Jews, find anti-Semitic feelings and attitudes in the Passion story. Jewish views are particularly influenced by the Holocaust. Some even go so far as to reinterpret the role of Caiaphas, making him out to be the defender of Jesus, who tried to save him from the Romans. They claim that the Passion narrative minimizes the responsibility of Pilate and increases that of the Jewish authorities. The texts themselves, however, clearly convey that Pilate is the one who condemned Jesus to death on the cross and that Romans carried out the sentence. The first-century Jewish historian Josephus wrote that Pilate condemned Jesus at the suggestion of "the principal men among us" (*Antiq.* 18, 63f). In the Passion narrative, the Temple authorities handed him over to the Romans as a dangerous rebel.

Historians will continue to analyze and interpret the Gospel Passion narratives and will express differing views about the historicity of Jesus' trial before the Sanhedrin that preceded the one before Pilate. They cannot dismiss the Gospel evidence that the main opponents of Jesus were Sadducees, who tried to preserve their privileged position in the Temple and collaborated with Roman rulers. Caiaphas' tenure as High Priest for an unusually long term (AD 18–36) can only be explained by his way of dealing with and pleasing the Romans. Modern New Testament scholars, who bring a sensible skepticism to their work and follow the evidence wherever it may lead, have convincingly argued that the cleansing of the Temple "persuaded the leaders of Judaism that this Galilean should not be allowed to create further trouble" [E. P. Sanders, *Jesus and Judaism* (Philadelphia: Fortress Press, 1985)]. This cleansing was much more than purification or reform of the Temple. Jesus' action was symbolic of its destruction. If the present Temple, therefore, is not final, then it follows that the Law, the basis of Temple worship, is not final. Jesus went beyond the Law and asserted his own authority. The conflict between Jesus and the Temple authorities led to his arrest and trials. To charge the Jews with guilt for the death of Jesus would be a simplistic interpretation of the text. The evangelists, as well as major modern critics, make a clear distinction between the hostility of the Temple authorities and the friendly concern of the people who sympathized with Jesus.

There is no doubt that the "anti-Jewish diatribes" in Matthew and John, removed from their context, have contributed to anti-Semitic hostile actions. Only within their historic context can we grasp their meaning. After a period of proclamation and preaching, these Gospels were written down following the destruction of the Temple. The Romans, by oppressive policies, provoked the people to open rebellion. In the wars that ensued, the Jews were severely punished and their Temple was destroyed. The new religious center in Jamnia, organized by the Pharisees, the only Jewish group that survived the first Jewish-Roman War, who started to draw boundaries around Judaism, separating Jews from Jewish Christians. They also changed a major prayer in the synagogues in a way that would exclude Christians from participating in them as places of worship. From this time forward, the conflict between them sharpened, leading to partition in the second century. Matthew and John faithfully transmit Jesus' life and ministry, as well as his suffering and death, ending with the Resurrection. At the same time, they reflect the period of disputes occurring when the Gospels were written. Generally speaking, we may say that they have a double perspective: that of the time of Jesus and of what was going on at their own time.

Commentators, both Christian and Jewish, have recognized that the language we find in Matthew 23 has roots in the Jewish tradition of disputes. The so-called "woes" are a common form of Jewish admonition. These passages, as well as Matthew 27.25, need a dispassionate analysis.

They reflect the bitter struggle between two groups who share the same heritage. Matthew condemns the Jamnian leaders and their interpretation of the common Jewish tradition in such a way as to exclude Jewish Christians from sharing in it.

Matthew did not fabricate Matthew 27.25, which belongs to the appearance before Pilate before the Crucifixion. The meaning of this verse is revealed in its larger context. During Jesus' public ministry, the Temple was an economic unit as well as a religious center. Thousands were engaged in Temple activities in some way. As we might expect, many of them would support the policy of the Temple leaders. That morning, when Caiaphas took Jesus to Pilate, they also accompanied him. The words shouted in the heat of the argument: "Let his blood be on us and on our children" should be ascribed to Temple dependents. The attitude of the Jewish people, on the other hand, differed sharply from that of Caiaphas and the Temple loyalists. They were friendly to Jesus, while the authorities feared that the people were with him. Matthew, as author of the above texts, has been accused as "the father of Christian anti-Semitism," but this accusation is clearly baseless. To remove the texts, as some have recommended, would not solve the problem. Interpreters, Jewish and Christian, must discuss them as family quarrels with the vitriol that was acceptable in their rhetorical tradition. Matthew was neither anti-Jewish nor anti-Semitic. He opposed the Pharisees in Jamnia, the new religious leaders of monolithic Judaism. Jesus too had disputes with Pharisees of an earlier time. Although some were friendly to him, this does not exclude his sharp criticism of the group.

John's Gospel also reflects the crisis between the Christian group and the leadership of the Pharisees. We should stress that only in this Gospel do we find the term *aposynagogos* (put out of the synagogue), not once but three times (9.22, 12.42, 16.2). By the time of John's Gospel, those who confessed that Jesus was the Messiah were treated as *minim* (heretics) and expelled from the synagogue. This exposed them to the threat of the Roman authorities. The Romans respected Judaism as an old traditional religion, but were suspicious of new cults and considered them troublesome to the Empire. The Christians, on the other hand, regarded themselves as heirs of an ancient tradition, not as members of a new cult.

The Fourth Gospel provides examples of harsh polemics with Jewish leaders. John charges that Jews follow their Law and "belong to the realm of darkness," language which recalls the language used by the Essenes against the Temple in Jerusalem. Matthew and John used language that was in no way unusual in intra-Jewish disputes. When we discuss the origin of Christian anti-Semitism, we must keep in mind that Jesus and the Twelve, the missionaries for the first twenty-five years, and the writers of the New Testament books, with one possible exception, were all of the race of Jews. There is no place for anti-Semitism in the New Testament, which enshrines the faith of the first two Christian generations. What brings hostility between Christians and Jews is misuse and misrepresentation of the Passion evidence.

Those who recorded the suffering and death of Jesus were witnesses to his Resurrection. His Resurrection illumines his Cross. The martyrs who followed him had only one desire: to imitate him and share in his passion, the Passion of their Lord. Their readiness for martyrdom was the fruit of their life in Christ. Their victory over death was his victory. In the memorable words of the second-century martyr Ignatius, "We are part of the fruit which grew out of his most blessed Passion" (*Smyr.* 1.2), and the followers of Christ have shown themselves as "branches of the Cross" (*Trall* 11.2).

The Passion of Christ

Behold, my servant shall prosper,
    he shall be exalted and lifted up,
        and shall be very high.
As many were astonished at him—
    his appearance was so marred,
        beyond human semblance,
    and his form beyond that of the sons of men—
so shall he startle many nations;
    kings shall shut their mouths
        because of him;
for that which has not been told them
        they shall see,
    and that which they have not
        heard they shall understand.

Who has believed what we have heard?
    And to whom has the arm of the Lord been revealed?
For he grew up before him like a young plant,
    and like a root out of dry ground;
he had no form or comeliness that we should look at him,
    and no beauty that we should desire him.

He was despised and rejected by men;
    a man of sorrows, and acquainted with grief;
and as one from whom men hide their faces
    he was despised, and we esteemed him not.

Surely he has borne our griefs and carried our sorrows;
    yet we esteemed him stricken, smitten by God, and
            afflicted.
But he was wounded for our transgressions,
    he was bruised for our iniquities;
upon him was the chastisement that made us whole,
    and with his stripes we are healed.
All we like sheep have gone astray;
    we have turned everyone to his own way;
and the Lord has laid on him the iniquity of us all.

He was oppressed and he was afflicted,
    yet he opened not his mouth;
like a lamb that is led to the slaughter,
    and like a sheep that before its shearers is dumb,
    so he opened not his mouth.
By oppression and judgment he was taken away;
    and as for his generation, who considered
that he was cut off out of the land of the living,
    stricken for the transgression of my people?

And they made his grave with the wicked
    and with the rich man in his death,
although he had done no violence,
    and there was no deceit in his mouth.

Yet it was the will of the Lord to bruise him;
    he has put him to grief;
when he makes himself an offering for sin,
    he shall see his offspring, he shall prolong his days;
the will of the Lord shall prosper in his hand;
    he shall see the fruit of the travail of his soul and be
        satisfied;
by his knowledge shall the righteous one, my servant,
make many to be accounted righteous;
    and he shall bear their iniquities.
Therefore I will divide him a portion with the great,
    and he shall divide the spoil with the strong;
because he poured out his soul to death,
    and was numbered with the transgressors;
yet he bore the sin of many,
    and made intercession for the transgressors.

                       Isaiah 52.13–53.12

I

"The Suffering Servant":
Prophecy and Fulfillment

IN HIS LIFE and particularly in his passion, Jesus of Nazareth fulfilled the role of the Suffering Servant of the Old Testament prophecies. In the Gospel accounts of Jesus' life, there are many clear references to this prophecy from Isaiah. In particular the passages referring to the death that awaits him in Jerusalem indicate that Jesus deliberately refers to his mission as the "Suffering Servant." Therefore we must be acquainted with the role ascribed to the Suffering Servant in the Old Testament.

In the book of the prophet Isaiah, we have four passages, known as the songs of the Suffering Servant of the Lord, which represent the highest point of Old Testament theology. These songs are given in Isaiah 42.1–4, 49.1–6, 50.4–9, and 52.13–53.12. Here we have a description of one who is elected, separated, for God's special purposes. He is not elected for privileges but for service and responsibility. His glory comes from the fact that he is in God's service and that he is elected to a worldwide mission and to suffering. God's spirit is upon him and he will bring forth justice to the nations. The Servant will carry the light of final revelation to all the people, and in him and through him God's salvation will reach to the ends of the earth. In performing this mission, the Servant will know nothing but suffering. But he will not be rebellious, he will not turn back. He will not hide his face "from shame and spitting." The prophet in his prediction goes on to assert the unshakable confidence of the Servant that God is with him, that he helps him, and, finally, that God will vindicate his Servant.

In the first three songs, it is not always clear when the prophecy refers to God's people, Israel, and when it points to an individual. Sometimes it seems that the people who are in God's possession will carry out the mission of the Servant, and sometimes it seems to be a particular individual, the Servant of God, who will bring the light to Israel as well as to the other nations. However, the fourth and final song speaks clearly to one person, whose sufferings are not simply the consequence of his mission but an essential part of it. Through suffering and only through suffering can his mission be accomplished. In the Orthodox Church this prophecy, Is 52.13–53.12, is always read on Good Friday. The Servant of this song points to Jesus of Nazareth. Only the Christ of the Gospels has fulfilled the role of the Suffering Servant of God. In several episodes in the Gospel narrative the evangelists indicate that the role of the Servant is fulfilled in the person of Jesus.

Let us now deal with the main events in the Gospels that refer to the theme of the servant in the Prophet Isaiah, the events which belong to Jesus' ministry before his entry into Jerusalem. This discussion will prepare us for a better understanding of the passion narrative itself.

The suffering of Christ started immediately after his birth, when Herod wanted to destroy him. At the beginning of his life, we find a king who was afraid of him as a little child, and at the end of his earthly ministry he suffers again at the hands of a man, the emperor's representative, who sentenced him to death on the cross.

Between the time of Herod and that of Pilate, we have the life of the Suffering Christ, and several episodes in his life refer to the suffering Servant of God. These are:

> 1. The Baptism and the Temptation of Christ
> 2. Jesus' rejection at Nazareth
> 3. The first prediction of the Passion
> 4. The Transfiguration of Christ, and the
>   second prediction of the Passion
> 5. The third prediction of the Passion.

The Baptism and the Temptation of Christ

In his Baptism in the Jordan (Mt 3.13–17; Mk 1.9–11; Lk 3.21–22; Jn 1.32–34), Jesus "was numbered with the transgressors" (Is 53.12). "For surely it is not with angels that he is concerned but with the descendants of Abraham" (Heb 2.16). At the beginning of his public ministry he is in company with those whom he would deliver from their sins. He is called Jesus, "for he will save his people from their sins" (Mt 1.21; Lk 2.21). At the end of his public ministry, he was crucified with two criminals. While one of the criminals was saying: "Are you not the Christ? Save yourself and us!", the other rebuked him, saying, "Do not you fear God, since you are under the same sentence of condemnation?

And we indeed justly; for we are receiving the due reward of our deeds; but this man has done nothing wrong." Then he asked Jesus to remember him when he came into his kingly power, and Jesus promised him that he would be with him in Paradise that very day (Lk 23.32–43). Jesus, although sinless, was baptized for the salvation of humanity, and he died on the cross, again for the salvation of humanity.

His baptism points to his passion and his death. Its full meaning is revealed in the voice which came from heaven, "You are my beloved Son, in whom I am well pleased." This divine proclamation, showing who Jesus is, combines the messianic Psalm 2.7 with the first verse of the first song of the Suffering Servant of God in Is 42.1. In this event of the baptism, two aspects of his person are made manifest. First, Jesus, on whom the Spirit descended like a dove, had a unique relationship with the Father and the Spirit. He is not inspired by the Spirit, as the prophets had been, but he possesses the Spirit permanently. He is the beloved Son. Second, it is the Servant of God himself who is present in the waters of the Jordan. In the fourth Gospel, John the Baptist pointed to Jesus with the words: "Behold, the Lamb of God, who takes away the sins of the world" (Jn 1.29). And again, when he was standing with two of his disciples and looking at Jesus, he said, "Behold the Lamb of God" (Jn 1.35). Aramaic scholars tell us that in the Aramaic, the language which Jesus and John the Baptist spoke, "the Lamb of God" means both "the Lamb of God" and "the Servant of God." In this reference to the sacrificial Lamb, John points to Christ's mission, which is to suffer for the sins of others and to die for his people.

Therefore Jesus' baptism anticipated the Cross. The church has recognized this from the beginning, and early pilgrims recounted that a cross was erected at the place where Jesus had been baptized. At the liturgical service of Epiphany, which marks Christ's baptism, a cross is plunged into the water at the time of the consecration of the waters.

During his temptation Jesus is asked to take a short cut to Paradise, to avoid the pain and suffering involved in his work for humanity's salvation. He is tempted to capture the hearts of people with signs and wonders. The devil wanted him, in other words, to be a false Christ (Mk 13.22). He challenged Christ with the words: "If you are the Son of God, command these stones to become loaves of bread," to which Jesus answered: "Man shall not live by bread alone, but by every word that proceeds from the mouth of God." In the second temptation, the devil asked him to throw himself from the pinnacle of the Temple, for the angels would take charge of him and would bear him up "lest you strike your foot against a stone." Jesus answered: "You shall not tempt the Lord your God." With these words Jesus opposed the rebellion of the devil and remained faithful and obedient. He overcame the tempter and proved himself to be the Son of God, the suffering Messiah, as the voice from heaven had announced at his baptism. Jesus is not a wonder maker but the obedient fulfiller of his mission, which is expressed in voluntary suffering. In the third temptation (Mt 4.8–10), the devil showed him all the kingdoms of the world and their glory and promised that he would give everything to Jesus if he would fall down and worship him (the devil). Jesus answered, "Be gone, Satan! for it is written: 'You shall worship the Lord your God, and him only shall you serve.'" Here also Jesus showed that he was the Son of God, for the prince of this world has no power over him (Jn 14.30).

St Luke in his Gospel, 4.1–13, ends his account of the temptation of Jesus with the following words: "And when the devil had ended every temptation, he departed from him until an opportune time." Clearly he had some other temptations of Jesus in mind. It has been suggested with strong justification that the essence of Satan's temptation would be horror of the passion that lay before him.

The Baptism tells us of the suffering Messiah; the Temptation points out that Jesus is ready to fulfill his mission and that all attempts of the devil to break his solidarity with his people are doomed to failure.

His Rejection at Nazareth

After the Baptism and the Temptation, Jesus came "in the power of the Spirit" into Galilee and here proclaimed the good news, the gospel of God. "The time is fulfilled, and the kingdom of God is at hand; repent and believe in the gospel" (Mk 1.15). One day he came to Nazareth, "where he had been brought up; and he went to the synagogue, as his custom was, on the Sabbath day." There he was given the book of the Prophet Isaiah to read. He found this passage and started to read:

> "The Spirit of the Lord is upon me
> because he has anointed me to preach good news to the poor.
> He has sent me to proclaim release to the captives,

and recovering of sight to the blind,
to set at liberty those who are oppressed,
to proclaim the acceptable year of the Lord." (Is 61)

When he finished reading, he closed the book and sat down;
"and the eyes of all in the synagogue were fixed on him" Then he
said to his congregation: "Today this scripture has been fulfilled
in your hearing." Isaiah 61 recalls the songs of the Suffering Servant. Here again, in the synagogue at Nazareth, is the Servant of
the Lord, whose divine power will be seen in the preaching of
the good news, and in the performance of mighty works. He was
not simply a messenger of the good news, but he had inaugurated the Messianic age.

It is unmistakably clear from Luke 4 that the people received
Jesus' proclamation of the kingdom of God with excitement.
"And all spoke well of him, and wondered at the gracious words
which proceeded out of his mouth" (Lk 4.22). But this group was
unable to understand him fully. They still looked upon him as
Joseph's son, and they could not see him as the Son of God. Their
question, "Is not this Joseph's son?" contains all their injured feelings, their pride and their unbelief: the man whose father and
mother they had known could not in their estimation hold such
an exalted position in God's plan for the Salvation of his people.
From their admiration of Jesus to their hostility toward him, it
was a short step. "He came to his own home, and his own people received him not" (Jn 1.11).

The First Prediction of the Passion

After feeding the multitude and healing the blind man of Bethsaida, Jesus with his disciples "came into the district of Caesarea
Philippi" and here for the first time he asked his disciples, "'Who
do men say that the Son of Man is?' And they said, 'Some say
John the Baptist, others say Elijah, and others Jeremiah or one
of the prophets.' He said to them, 'But who do you say that I
am?'" Then Peter, in the name of the disciples, answered, "You
are the Christ, the Son of the living God" (Mt 16.13–23; Mk
8.27–33; Lk 9.18–22; Jn 6.66–69). Peter's confession is followed
by Christ's first prediction of the Passion. Jesus began to teach
them that he must go to Jerusalem and that "The Son of Man
must suffer many things, and be rejected by the elders and the
chief priests and the scribes, and be killed, and after three days
rise again" (Mk 8.31, Mt 16.21, Lk 9.22). Peter did not like this
prophecy. He had confessed him to be the Christ, and he did not
expect that Christ must die. The apostle even rebuked Jesus, saying to him, "God forbid, Lord! This shall never happen to you"
(Mt. 16.22). Peter expressed his terror of suffering, and not only
Peter but all the other disciples misunderstood the meaning of
Jesus' Messiahship. For this reason he reprimanded Peter for try-
ing to persuade him from the path of suffering. It is significant
that before Jesus addressed Peter with harsh words: "Get behind
me, Satan! For you are not on the side of God, but of men"
(Mt 16.23; Mk 8.23), he turned to look at his disciples ("but turn-
ing and seeing his disciples, he rebuked Peter"), because Peter
expressed their thoughts too. In Jesus' rebuke of Peter, there is an

echo of the temptations which Jesus had undergone in the wilderness.

The passage that we are discussing now represents the watershed in the Gospel narrative. After Peter's confession, Jesus started in unmistakable terms to teach his disciples about his suffering to come. First of all, Jesus accepts Peter's confession; he is the Messiah (the Hebrew word for Christ). He is the Messiah, just because he must suffer. This was not expected by the Jews. For them, the Messiah had a political role to perform. Jesus freed the concept of the Messiah from its national and political aspects and represented it as purely religious. The nature of his Messiahship would be unambiguously expressed in his confrontation with Pilate, when he told the Roman representative, "My kingdom is not of this world" (Jn 18.36).

As we have seen from the first prediction of the passion, Jesus referred to himself as "the Son of Man." After Peter confesses that he is the Messiah, the title is interpreted in terms of Messianic suffering. The name "the Son of Man," found always in the Gospels on Jesus' lips, at times depicts his humility and at times his divine sovereignty. Therefore this name is the most comprehensive, namely, the Messiah who has come is both human and divine.

This Son of Man would be rejected by the elders, the chief priests, and the scribes. These three groups, mentioned explicitly in the first prediction of the Passion, are the ones who constitute the Sanhedrin, the supreme Jewish ruling body. The name Sanhedrin comes from the Greek *sunedrion*, meaning "court." In view of the decisive role of the Sanhedrin in removing Jesus from the historical scene, let us identify these three groups. The *elders* were the leading lay members of the socially most prominent families in Jerusalem. The *chief priests* included the high priest, who held the office, the former high priests still living, and the most important priests performing duties in the Temple. The chief priests and elders represented the attitudes of the Sadducees, the wealthy landowners and aristocracy of Jerusalem. The Sadducees accepted only the first five books of Moses as their Scripture and were suspicious of everything new. They regarded any new teaching or revelation as a threat to their political and economic power. They always tried to compromise with the power of Rome in order to preserve their privileges. The third group in the Sanhedrin was composed of the *Scribes*, the teachers and scholars of the law. A modern scholar has called them "the Ph.D.'s of their time." In the Sanhedrin they represented the Pharisaic school of thought. The Pharisees were attached to the law and the oral interpretation of the law. Their influence among the people was great, for they were connected with the synagogues.

The Transfiguration of Christ, and the Second Prediction of the Passion

In the Transfiguration, the confession at Caesarea Philippi and Jesus' first prediction of his Passion receive divine confirmation. In the presence of Peter, James, and John, Jesus was transfigured and his three disciples were privileged to see him in glory; God's glory, what had always been with him, was now revealed. On the mount of the Transfiguration, Moses and Elijah appeared and were talking to Jesus. In St Luke's account of the Transfiguration, we read that they "spoke of his departure, which he was to accomplish in Jerusalem" (Lk 9.31). The Greek word that the Evangelist uses in this verse and that is translated into English as "departure" is the word *exodus*. This word is used for death in the early Christian literature, as well as in the Lukan narrative of the Transfiguration. In Jerusalem Jesus would perform another exodus, and through this exodus, his death, he would deliver his people from the slavery of sin. Thus again, the Messiah, who had shown his divine glory, must suffer, and the inner circle of the disciples must be taught once again about the divine necessity of this suffering. Jesus' acceptance of this suffering is not by blind necessity; it is the will of God. And this will, he made his own. As Jesus was to say at Gethsemane, "Not what I will, but what you will."

In the account of the Transfiguration, the voice that came out of the cloud—"This is my beloved Son; listen to him"—recalls the voice at the Baptism. It is the link between the Baptism, the Transfiguration, and the Passion of Christ in Jerusalem.

At the time of Jesus' transfiguration, the three apostles "were exceedingly afraid" (Mk 9.6). After hearing the voice say, "listen to him," meaning "listen to him all the time, always," the disciples no longer reject Jesus' suffering. When Jesus for the second time made a prediction of his passion with the words, "The Son of Man will be delivered into the hands of men, and they will kill him; and when he is killed, after three days he will rise," the disciples did not protest, "but they did not understand the saying, and they were afraid to ask him" (Mk 9.32; Mt 17.22–23; Lk 9.43–45).

In the second prophecy of the Passion, the term "the Son of Man" is used again. He also will come at the end as the judge of the world is now to be rejected and killed by men.

The Third Prediction of the Passion

Jesus and his disciples were on the way to Jerusalem. Conscious of his mission as the Suffering Christ, he was leading them, and they were amazed and afraid. There in the Holy City, in the center of the religious and political life of Jerusalem, he was to meet his opposition. Jesus had twice prophesied the outcome of this confrontation. They had heard these predictions, and therefore were filled with fear seeing Jesus, who "was walking ahead of them" toward Jerusalem. Jesus again started to tell the Twelve what would happen to him.

"Behold, we are going up to Jerusalem; and the Son of Man will be delivered to the chief priests and the scribes, and they will condemn him to death, and deliver him to the Gentiles; and they will mock him, and spit upon him, and scourge him, and kill him; and after three days he will rise" (Mt 20.17–19; Mk 10.32–34; Lk 18.31–34).

If we compare and analyze the three predictions of the Passion, we may observe that although all three contain the same essential revelation about the rejection and death of the Son of Man, they differ in the gradual disclosure of details. In the first prophecy, Jesus pointed to his main enemy, the Sanhedrin. The second prediction implies that Gentiles as well as Jews would be responsible for his death, for he would be delivered "into the hands of men." And finally the third prophecy is quite explicit about what is implied in the second and it completes the first one. According to the third prediction, the representatives of the two most influential groups, the Sadducees and the Pharisees, would condemn Jesus to death and afterward would deliver him to the Romans. And who could the Gentiles in Jerusalem be if not the Romans? There are also details in the last prediction which describe how Jesus would be treated during his trial before Rome's representative, when he would be mocked, spat upon, and scourged.

It is interesting to compare the reactions of the disciples to the three predictions. After the first, Peter, speaking also for the others, rebuked Jesus for speaking about such horrible things. Having heard the second, they were afraid to say anything. And after the third, St Luke records their reaction in the following way: "But they understood none of these things; his saying was hid from them and they did not grasp what was said." We may also add that all three prophecies were spoken in the presence of all the Twelve, and all encountered great difficulties in understanding and accepting Jesus' foretelling of his death. They were still under the spell of the popular expectation held by the Jews that the Messiah would come to restore the kingdom to Israel.

These three predictions are given within the framework of two miracles. Prior to Peter's confession and the first prediction, there is the record of how Jesus healed a blind man at Bethsaida (Mk 8.22–26), and after the third prediction there is another miracle of restoring sight to the blind beggar, Bartimaeus, just at the time Jesus was leaving Jericho and finally approaching Jerusalem

(Mk 10.46–52). Between these two mighty works, Jesus was try-ing to open the spiritual eyes of the disciples, that they might understand that the Son of Man had come "not to be served but to serve, and to give his life as ransom for many" (Mk 10.45). Redemption would be achieved by and through death and his death would be for the salvation of all. The expression "for many" takes us back again to Isaiah 53.11–12 and is a Semitic, concrete way of saying that he would give his life for so many that you cannot number them, that is, for all. Here a sharp contrast is drawn; "The one" voluntarily gives his life for "the many." He, who is loved immensely by his Father and on whom the Spirit descended and remained, will be rejected and will suffer. Throughout his ministry he was guided by the Spirit, and with the Spirit of God he performed miracles. In every act as well as in every word he expressed the love of God and the pure will of God. The beloved Son (the adjective "beloved" is used eight times in the Gospels and each time it designates Jesus), with whom the Father is "well pleased," entered into Jerusalem and spent the last week of his public ministry there. It is at this point that the Passion narrative itself properly begins.

II

Christ's Ministry in Jerusalem

B EFORE HIS ENTRY into Jerusalem, Jesus had spoken openly
about the nature of his Messiahship only to his disciples,
as we have seen from our discussion of the three predictions of
the Passion. On the other hand, he veiled his role as the Messiah
from public knowledge. He imposed silence on any others who
professed him as the Messiah. He did not permit demons or
unclean spirits to speak about it, as he did not want them to
make him known (Mk 3.11–12). When he raised the daughter of
Jairus, he "strictly charged" the child's father and mother and
three of his disciples (Peter, James, and John) who were with him
where the child was, "that no one should know this, and told
them to give her something to eat" (Mk 5.35–43). He wanted to
avoid the enthusiasm of the crowd, which would not understand
him and his work. At one point in his ministry, immediately after
Jesus fed the five thousand, he was actually forced to flee from
the crowd, which in its excitement wanted to make him king.
"Perceiving then that they were about to come and take him by
force to make him king, Jesus withdrew again to the hills by himself" (Jn 6.15). The very word "again" implies that this was neither the first nor the only time that he withdrew for this reason.

In the example just quoted, he withdrew from a friendly crowd, but at the same time it was a crowd that could not perceive the inner meaning of the miracle Jesus had performed and could not understand who Jesus was.

After the Transfiguration, Jesus charged Peter, James, and John "to tell no one what they had seen, until the Son of Man should have risen from the dead. So they kept the matter to themselves" (Mk 9.9–10). To those who asked him, "Are you he who is to come, or shall we look for another?" Jesus offered the most concrete answer that could be given. He let his works speak for themselves: "The blind receive their sight and the lame walk, lepers are cleansed and the deaf hear, and the dead are raised up and the poor have good news preached to them. And blessed is he who takes no offense at me" (Mt 11.2–6). With the disciples he spoke openly and explicitly, but with others only in an indirect and a veiled form about the true nature of his mission.

With Jesus' entry into Jerusalem, the Passion narrative begins. It is a continuous narrative. If we read through St Mark's Gospel in one sitting, we have the impression that the evangelist is in a great hurry in the first ten chapters in order to come as soon as possible to Jesus' days in Jerusalem. At this point, he takes time and solemnly records day by day what Jesus said and did. By following the second canonical Gospel, we are able to have a clear outline of events in Jesus' ministry in Jerusalem. He entered the Holy City on the day following the Jewish Sabbath (Sunday). On the following day (Monday) he cleansed the Temple. In the evening he went out of the city with his disciples (Mk 11.19), "and in the morning" (Mk 11.20) they came again to

Jerusalem (Mk 11.27). On this day (Tuesday) Jesus discoursed with his opponents, answering their questions and teaching in parables. We shall deal with three of the questions addressed to him by the leading men of Israel and with one of his parables, as well as with his discourse about the impending catastrophe and the end of the present age. "Two days before the Passover" (Wednesday) (Mk 14.1) occurred the anointing at Bethany and the betrayal by Judas. On the day "when they sacrificed the Passover lamb" (Mk 14.12) and "when it was evening" (Thursday) we have the institution of the Lord's Supper. On "the day of Preparation, that is, the day before the Sabbath" (Mk 15.42) Jesus died on the cross. And when the Sabbath was past, "very early on the first day of the week . . . the women went to the tomb" (Mk 16.1–2) and found it empty. Although we shall not treat the Resurrection narrative in this pamphlet, we must constantly keep in mind that the Cross and the Resurrection are inseparable, and the Orthodox Church never separates them, as the hymnography clearly states: "We fall down before thy Cross, O Lord, and we sing and glorify thy Holy Resurrection." The Passion of Christ was never treated in the apostolic message apart from the Resurrection of Christ.

It is not so easy to discern in Matthew or Luke the outline that we find in the Gospel of St Mark. Although they are in full agreement on the essentials, they sometimes disagree on the chronological order of the events. Thus, according to St Matthew's Gospel, the cleansing of the Temple took place on the day that Jesus entered Jerusalem. St Luke's account agrees with this, but St John puts it at the beginning of Jesus' ministry. While they disagree here and in some other places regarding the chronology of certain events, they are in full agreement that they occurred and also on their theological meaning. Our salvation does not depend upon the chronology or the historical order of events, but it depends solely on what Christ did for us, what he is doing now, and on what he will do at his Second Coming. Although the establishment of a chronology of events is important for a better understanding of the Gospel records, it must be recognized that the Gospel writers were more preoccupied with the substance and its meaning than with distance, measurement, or chronology.

The Entry into Jerusalem

This triumphal event is recorded by all four evangelists (Mt 21.1–11; Mk 11.1–10; Lk 19.29–40; Jn 12.12–19). When Jesus was approaching Jerusalem with his disciples, he sent two of them to a nearby village where they would find as soon as they entered "a colt tied, on which no one had ever sat." They were asked to bring it to Jesus. If anyone asked them about untying this colt, they were to say, according to Jesus' instruction, "the Lord has need of it." Jesus quite deliberately fulfilled the prophecy of the prophet Zechariah of the sixth century BC:

> Rejoice greatly, O daughter of Zion!
> Shout aloud, O daughter of Jerusalem!
> Lo, your king comes to you;
> Triumphant and victorious is he,
> Humble and riding on an ass,
> On a colt, the foal of an ass (Zech 9.9).

Why did Jesus perform such acts? Now the time had come for an open, public declaration to everyone of his claim and the meaning of his own kingship and Messiahship. By entering Jerusalem seated upon an ass, an animal of peace, Jesus made known that he was the king, but a king who was not going to use the sword, for he was not the king of war but of peace, who came to accomplish God's purpose in the Holy City. His purpose was not to declare political rebellion against the Romans, but to establish a new relationship between God and man, to reconcile man with God and to bring peace between them.

According to St John, the disciples did not fully understand the meaning of Jesus' fulfillment of the prophecy from Zechariah. "But when Jesus was glorified, then they remembered that this had been written of him" (Jn 12.16). The crowds who cried "Hosanna!" understood it even less. Hosanna is the Hebrew word meaning "Save! Save now!" The great crowd had heard and knew what Jesus had done in Galilee, and in Judaea, particularly the raising of Lazarus (Jn 11), without comprehending what was conveyed by his entry into Jerusalem riding on an ass. The crowd was looking for another sort of king, who would be ready to use the sword if necessary. On this Sunday, Jerusalem was full of excitement, tension, and profoundly serious conflict between two different types of Messiahship. Jesus said one thing, but the crowd expected from him something else, quite opposite to that which Jesus had publicly proclaimed that day. The evangelists give us evidence of the struggle that was going on. Even in the joyful exclamation of the crowd, the conflict may be observed. St Matthew reports that "most of the crowd spread their garments on the road" (Mt 21.8, also Mk 11.8, "many spread their garments" and Lk 19.36). What is important in these reports is that "many" in the crowd wanted another sort of fulfillment from that prophesied by Zechariah 9.9. The crowd wanted Jesus to be a king like Jehu, from 2 Kings 9. In this chapter, men spread their garments before him, blew their trumpets, and proclaimed, "Jehu is King." This king was known as a revolutionary. The crowd wanted Jesus to fulfill his mission in a manner that would be similar to a war-king, to please them and fulfill their expectation and realize their nationalistic hopes.

When Jesus entered Jerusalem, St Matthew pointedly adds, the city was stirred, many asked "'Who is this?' and the crowds said, 'This is the prophet Jesus from Nazareth of Galilee'" (Mt 21.10–11). This verse indicates another contrast on the day of Jesus' entry into Jerusalem. For the crowds he was a prophet, whereas the apostle Peter had confessed at Caesarea Philippi that he was "the Christ, the Son of the living God." To Peter's confession Jesus had answered, "Blessed are you, Simon Bar-Jonah! For flesh and blood has not revealed this to you, but my Father who is in heaven" (Mt 16.17). The crowd does not have the faith of the disciples. Although the multitude and the disciples do not understand the real meaning of Jesus' entry into Jerusalem, their misunderstanding cannot be put on the same level and will not have the same consequences. In a few days the crowd will change its heart and will ask for the crucifixion of Jesus. The disciples will be frightened, will flee away, and Peter, the leader, will deny him, but at the end of this drama they will meet him again, proclaim him, and suffer for him. The crowd, as before, during his ministry in Galilee, admired Jesus and rejoiced in his works, but was far from following him.

Late on the Sunday of his entry, Jesus with his disciples left Jerusalem and went out to Bethany. This place "was near Jerusalem, about two miles off" (Jn 11.18). Bethany was the village of Lazarus, whom Jesus had raised up, and of Lazarus' two sisters, Mary and Martha. He did the same on Monday evening: "When evening came they went out of the city" (Mk 11.19), as well as on succeeding evenings. The third Gospel gives us a summary of how Jesus spent his days in Jerusalem: "Every day he was teaching in the temple, but at night he went out and lodged in the mount called Olivet. And early in the morning all the people came to him in the temple to hear him" (Lk 21.37–38). Bethany is included in the region of Olivet. These references to Jesus' leaving the city in the evening and spending the night outside it are clear evidence of the hostile intentions of his opponents in the city.

The Cleansing of the Temple

"On the following day" (Mk 11.12), that is, on Monday, on his way with the Twelve from Bethany to Jerusalem, Jesus was hungry, and seeing in the distance a fig tree he came to it but "found nothing but leaves." Then he pronounced the judgment on this fig tree: "May no one ever eat fruit from you again." He did it in spite of the fact that "it was not the season for figs" (Mk 11.13–14). Next morning when they passed by, the Twelve saw "the fig tree withered away to its roots" (Mk 11.20). This is a miracle, and the evangelist wants us to see it as a miracle and not as an enacted parable.

This miracle belongs to Jesus' ministry of the Passion Week. Like every other miracle of Jesus, it expresses what actually happened and also points to a meaning beyond itself.

What is the meaning of this miracle? The fig tree is used in the Old Testament to symbolize Israel. Sometimes it is employed as an image of Israel's indifference, negligence, and unfaithfulness. According to the prophet Jeremiah, for example, the kingdom of Judah is like a vine or a fig tree that does not bring any fruit and therefore destruction will fall upon it (Jer 8.13–17). Even earlier is Hosea, whose prophetic ministry belongs to the eighth century BC, and who employed the image of the fig tree for Israel:

> "Like grapes in the wilderness
>> I found Israel,
> Like the first fruit on the fig tree in its first season
>> I saw your fathers" (Hos 9.10).

In the light of these and other references, the miracle of the fig tree points to Jesus' judgment on contemporary Judaism. Its outside appearance, its observances and ceremonies, are like "a fig tree in leaf." But, like the fig tree of the miracle, it is barren. Although "it was not the season for figs," this tree had not produced even the small knobs or early green figs that would have been a sure sign that the tree was fruitful. Sometimes a hungry man would eat those early figs to satisfy his hunger.

The miracle of the withered fig tree is followed by another dramatic event, Jesus' entry into the Temple with the purpose not simply of observing what is going on in it but of cleansing it. Jesus entered the Temple and drove out the buyers and the ven-

dors. All four evangelists agree that he exercised divine authority in performing this cleansing. He told the vendors, "Take
these things away; you shall not make my Father's house a house
of trade" (Jn 2.16). The trade was with animals and wine, and the
money changers were receiving their fee for their services. This
market in the Temple was under the control of the chief priests
and other members of the ruling body. The act of Jesus had universal implications. He said to those who were engaged in this
trade, "Is it not written, 'My house shall be called a house of
prayer for all the nations'? But you have made it a den of robbers"
(Mk 11.17). Jesus was not against worship in the Temple as such,
nor was he simply seeking to reform it; his mission was to make
a complete transformation of it into a form of worship in which
Gentiles would participate. The new Temple, "the temple of his
body" (Jn 2.21) would include "all nations." This was the fulfillment of Isaiah's prophecy 56.7. According to the prophet Isaiah,
the messianic age would be inaugurated when Gentiles wor-
shipped with Jews. With the coming of the Messiah, in other
words, Jewish worship would be transformed into a universal
worship. If the scene of the cleansing of the Temple occurred in
the part known as the Court of Gentiles, which was separated
from other parts of the Temple edifice, and it is highly probable
that it happened there, then Jesus by his actions indicates that he
came to remove the dividing wall that separates the Gentiles
from other but more central divisions of the Temple, where only
Jews were allowed. A non-Jew could not go beyond the Court of
Gentiles. Jesus, however, includes this court in "my house" also.
This Court of Gentiles should be a place of prayer as well, he

implies. There are four accounts of the cleansing of the Temple, one in each of the Gospels, but not a single one indicates that Jesus was angry, either when he entered the Temple or when he expelled those who traded in the Temple.

The cleansing of the Temple was a "dangerous act," yet it was the work of the Messiah. Jesus did not simply criticize what was going on in the Temple, but he cleansed it. Jeremiah almost lost his life for prophesying that the Temple by itself would not assure God's presence and protection. In his so-called "Temple Sermon," he proclaimed the word that had come to him from the Lord: the Temple would be destroyed if the people did not experience moral change (Jer 7.1–15 and 26.7–15). In addition to Is 56.7, Christ referred to Jer 7.11 at the time of the cleansing of the Temple: "Has this house which is called by my name become a den of robbers in your eyes?" By this reference of Jeremiah, Christ may have had in mind the suffering that he too would undergo for his action in the Temple.

The reaction of the "chief priests and the scribes and the principal men of the people" (the Sanhedrin) was immediate. They "sought a way to destroy him" (Lk 19.47; Mk 11.18). Before that, they had another task to perform; to separate the masses of the people from Jesus and his influence. They realized that "all the multitude was astonished at his teaching" (Mk 11.18). The people were listening attentively to Jesus' words and were look-ing approvingly upon his acts. The members of the ruling body, for the time being, "did not find anything they could do, for all the people hung upon his words" (Lk 19.48). For this reason they decided to try to discredit Jesus, to compromise him in the eyes of the people, and then to destroy him physically without fear of the multitude. They planned to trap him with three questions: the question of authority, the question of tribute to Caesar, and the question about the Resurrection.

The Three Questions

The question about the authority was asked by the members of the Sanhedrin. The chief priests and the scribes and the elders came up to him as he was walking in the Temple and they said to him, "By what authority are you doing these things, and who gave you this authority to do them?" "These things" refers primarily to the cleansing of the Temple. Jesus answered their question by a counter-question: "Was the baptism of John from heaven or from men?" The leading members argued among themselves. If they said that the baptism of John was from heaven, they were quite sure that Jesus would ask them a second question, "Why then did you not believe him?" If they said that John's baptism was from men, they were afraid of the reaction of the people, "for all held that John was a real prophet." Finally they agreed among themselves to answer the question with a negative, noncommittal answer, "We do not know." They believed this answer would protect them from any possible attack or accusation, either from Jesus or from the people. In response to their answer, Christ simply said, "Neither will I tell you by what authority I do these things" (Mt 21.23–27; Mk 11.27–33; Lk 20.1–8).

The delegation from the Sanhedrin asked about legal authority. They were interested in authority that is based upon the law. In his answer, Jesus lifted the problem of authority to a different level. He went beyond their question and pointed to the real source of authority, to God. "By what authority?" in the question of the Sanhedrin's delegate meant which legal body authorized you, or on the basis of which law did you do "these things." In his counter-question, Jesus claimed that his authority comes from heaven, or God, as "heaven" stands for the name God. At the same time he rejected the right of the delegates from the Sanhedrin to set themselves as his judges in order to verify his credentials, and he reminded them that they had rejected the call of the prophet, John the Baptist, for repentance. From the very beginning of his public ministry, the people "were astonished at his teaching, for he taught them as one who had authority, and not as the scribes" (Mk 1.22). The authority of the Scribes was of a derivative character, legal authority. They studied the work and opinion of previous teachers, and on the basis of their teaching, which again was of a derivative nature, they formed their own opinion.

By not answering the question about his authority directly, Jesus was judging and revealing the real intentions of the religious leaders. Above all, he judged them for separating the law from God, and thus concealing God behind the Law. This judgment had first been pronounced in the miracle of the fig tree, then in the cleansing of the Temple, and now in the dispute over authority. The first question of the delegates from the Sanhedrin did not produce desirable results for them.

After this initial failure, the Sanhedrin sent to Jesus "some of the Pharisees and some of the Herodians, to entrap him in his talk" (Mk 12.13; Mt 22.15). They raised the question concerning tribute to Caesar: "Teacher, we know that you are true, and care for no man; for you do not regard the position of men, but truly teach the way of God. Is it lawful to pay taxes to Caesar, or not? Should we pay them or should we not?" The coin had the likeness of Caesar, "Render to Caesar the things that are Caesar's," said Jesus. The human being, on the other hand, is created in the image and likeness of God. "Render to God the things that are God's."

This episode is important for several reasons. The Pharisees and the Herodians were on good terms only when they plotted against Jesus. Even earlier, when Jesus was in Galilee, the Pharisees had held counsel with the Herodians as to how to destroy him (Mk 3.6). Otherwise the Pharisees did not care for the Herodians, the political supporters of Herod Antipas, nor did the Herodians think highly about the religious party of the Pharisees. At the beginning and the end of Jesus' ministry, however, they worked together. Now they approached Jesus, not with the arrogance of the members of the Sanhedrin, but seemingly with sincerity and politeness. They pretended, however, to be sincere "that they might take hold of what he said, so as to deliver him up to the authority and jurisdiction of the governor" (Lk 20.20). The real reason for their question is precisely stated here. The tax in question had been imposed by the Romans in the provinces. A political group in Palestine, known as the Zealots, opposed paying this tax and was known as the Anti-Roman Party. They did not shrink from the use of violence either. Jesus' questioners hoped to connect him with the Zealots, accuse him to the Romans as a revolutionary, and in this way to get rid of him. Christ, however, regarded the views advocated by the Zealots as a satanic understanding of the Messiah. They regarded the kingdom of God as identical with the form of the state. Political domination was their aim.

This story may be considered a reflection of the third temptation of Christ in the wilderness. This narrative also alludes to national political affairs. The current ideals of the time are pictured in a metaphorical way in the temptation record. As Stephen Liberty wrote in *The Political Relations of Christ's Ministry* (London: B.H. Milford, Oxford University Press, 1916), the Sadducees represent "the love of ease," the Pharisees "the arrogance towards God," and the Herodians "readiness for apostasizing compromise with the heathen world." In the first temptation we have an allusion to the Sadducees, in the second to the Pharisees, and in the third to the Herodians. In addition to these groups, we have Jesus' fight with the extreme nationalists, the Zealots. In the devil's offering of the kingdoms of this world and the glory of them, Jesus also saw the ideal of the Zealots. He made a clear distinction between the kingdom of God and the kingdom of man, between "the things that are God's" and "the things that are Caesar's."

The questioners, therefore, approached Jesus in a hostile spirit. As soon as they raised their question about the lawfulness of paying taxes to Caesar, Jesus was aware of their "malice" and "hypocrisy." "He perceived their craftiness" and said to them, "Why put me to the test?" (Mt 22.18; Mk 12.15; Lk 20.23). When they heard his answer, "they were amazed at him" (Mk 12.17, Mt 22.22). For his reply was to "put God above everything else, the ultimate loyalty belongs only to him." The Pharisees and the Herodians failed "in the presence of the people to catch him by what he said" (Lk 20.26). They were silent and went way.

After the Pharisees, some Sadducees came to him. They were members of the priestly aristocracy, as we have previously mentioned, and the high priest belonged to this party. They did not believe in resurrection, and with their question they intended to "reduce to the absurd" the belief in resurrection. They proposed the case of a woman who was married; her husband died and they were childless. According to the Law of Moses, she married her husband's brother (Deut 25.5, "if brothers dwell together, and one of them dies and has no son, the wife of the dead shall not be married outside the family to a stranger; her husband's brother shall go in to her, and take her as his wife, and perform the duty of a husband's brother to her"). And the second brother died, leaving no children. There were seven brothers. In each case, the same thing happened. After the death of the seventh brother, the woman also died. The Sadducees were interested in knowing, "In the Resurrection whose wife will she be? For the seven had her as wife" (Mt 22.23–28; Mk 12.18–23; Lk 20.27–33). In answering them, Jesus indicated what was wrong with the questioners. "You know neither the resurrection nor the power of God." The Sadducees accepted as their Scriptures the Pentateuch, the first five books of the Old Testament. It is precisely in these books, according to Christ, that belief in resurrection is not simply implied but demanded. "And as for the dead being raised, have you not read in the book of Moses, in the passage about the bush, how God said to him, 'I am the God of Abraham, and the

God of Isaac, and the God of Jacob'? He is not the God of the dead, but of the living; you are quite wrong." The Sadducees did not believe in the Resurrection, whereas the Pharisees did, and the crowds were mainly under their influence. Not only did the Sadducees reveal their ignorance regarding their own Scripture, but they also showed that they were absolutely wrong about "the power of God." They applied the categories of this life to the life to come. They put the life in this world on the same level with the life in the kingdom of God. Their qualitative difference was completely confused. Therefore Jesus said to him: "When they rise from the dead, they neither marry nor are given in marriage, but are like angels in heaven" (Mk 12.25; Mt 22.30; Lk 20.35).

Jesus' answers are not simply answers to his opponent's questions. In each answer he leads men to the kingdom of God, and gives a new teaching. The crowd was astonished at his teaching; his enemies "no longer dared to ask him any questions" (Mt. 22.33, Lk 20.40).

The Parable of the Wicked Tenants

Between the controversy about authority and the question concerning tribute to Caesar, we find in the Gospel narrative the parable of the wicked tenants. It is part of the struggle that Jesus had with the Temple authorities in Jerusalem. It puts the conflict expressed in the three questions into sharper focus, for in telling it, Jesus is taking the initiative and is revealing an event that soon will take place. The parable is recorded by the first three evangelists (Mt 21.33–46; Mk 12.1–12; Lk 20.9–19).

And he began to speak to them in parables. "A man planted a vineyard, and set a hedge around it, and dug a pit for the wine press, and built a tower, and let it out to tenants, and went into another country. When the time came, he sent a servant to the tenants, to get from them some of the fruit of the vineyard. And they took him and beat him, and sent him away empty-handed. Again he sent to them another servant, and they wounded him in the head, and treated him shamefully. And he sent another, and him they killed; and so with many others, some they beat and some they killed. He had still one other, a beloved son; finally he sent him to them, saying 'They will respect my son.' But those tenants said to one another, 'this is the heir; come, let us kill him, and the inheritance will be ours.' And they took him and killed him, and cast him out of the vineyard. What will the owner of the vineyard do? He will come and destroy the tenants, and give the vineyards to others. Have you not read this scripture:

"The very stone which the builders rejected
Has become the head of the corner;
This was the Lord's doing,
And it is marvelous in our eyes?"

And they tried to arrest him, but feared the multitude, for they perceived that he had told the parable against them; so they left him and went away.

In this parable Jesus gives us the story of Israel and relates his ministry to it. In a summary form it records what God did for his people, and what the people did to his messengers, to his prophets. Finally God sent his beloved Son. God (the owner of the vineyard), Israel (the vineyard), its tenants (the leaders), and a beloved Son (Jesus) are the main figures in the drama of salvation. The Epistle to the Hebrews makes the same point in its opening verses: "In many and various ways God spoke of old to our fathers by the prophets; but in these last days he has spoken to us by a Son" (Heb 1.1–2). The parable has an autobiographic character. In the same week in which the parable was spoken, the beloved Son (Jesus) would be condemned to death by the tenants (the religious leaders). In a few days the parable became history. In this story Jesus spoke about his own death and made the ruling body responsible for it. He warned them that by rejecting him they would forfeit their claim to the vineyard. The church would be built upon the rejected stone, and the beloved Son would become its foundation as well as its head.

In St Mark's Gospel, the name "beloved Son" is used three times only, first at the Baptism of Jesus, second at his Transfiguration, and third, here in the parable of the wicked tenants. In the events as well as in the parable, Jesus is identified as the beloved Son of God. First, God himself proclaimed it to the people and the disciples, and then Jesus identified himself with the beloved Son when he uttered the parable in Jerusalem in the presence of his main opponents. All three episodes show that Jesus knew that he was the beloved Son and that he would be the suffering Son, the crucified Messiah.

The "tenants" understood that the parable was told to them and against them, and still they were only concerned with his removal. When they heard the parable, they reacted in the same way as they had when they saw Jesus cleansing the Temple. Here again the scribes and the chief priests tried to arrest him, but they did not dare to do so. They feared the people, "because they held him to be a prophet" (Mt 21.46). Hence this parable, as well as the cleansing of the Temple, leads us directly to the Passion.

Discourse about Coming Events

When Jesus was leaving the Temple, his disciples remarked on its beauty and grandeur. Jesus responded with a prediction of the Temple's destruction: "Do you see these great buildings? There will not be left here one stone upon another that will not be thrown down" (Mk 13.2; Mt 24.2; Lk 21.6). After he reached the Mount of Olives with the Twelve to spend the night outside Jerusalem—for Jerusalem "killed the prophets and stoned those who are sent" to it (Mt 23.37, Lk 13.34)—Peter, James, John, and Andrew "asked him privately" when the destruction of the Temple would occur and what sign would precede it.

A few days before his public ministry ended, Jesus spoke of the future with his disciples. First of all, he warned them that many would come in his name in order to lead them astray. These imposters would succeed with many people and would be accepted by many, but, he tells the disciples, "Do not go after them" (Lk 21). "Nation will rise against nation, and kingdom against kingdom; there will be earthquakes in various places, there will be famines; this is but the beginning of sufferings" (Mk 13.8; Mt 24.7; Lk 21.22). The disciples of Jesus would suffer many things, would be delivered up to councils, and beaten in synagogues, and would stand before governors and kings "for my sake, to bear testimony before them." Before their accusers and torturers they would say what would be given them to say by the Holy Spirit, "for it is not you who speak, but the spirit of your Father speaking through you" (Mt 24.20; Mk 13.11). "I will give you a mouth and wisdom which none of your adversaries will be able to withstand or contradict," said Jesus, according to St Luke's Gospel. As at the beginning of this period of trial and torment imposters would appear to mislead the people, so at the climax they would appear again. They are identified as "false Christs and false prophets" (Mk 13.21), who would perform "signs and wonders to lead astray, if possible, the elect."

In three chapters found in the first three Gospels (Mt 24, Mk 13, and Lk 21) Jesus discourses about events that will take place in the future. Jesus, first of all, refers to a historical crisis in the near future, the destruction of the Holy City. Second, he speaks about the ultimate consummation of the present age that would come at the end. Often these two events are merged and are not separated from each other, for what is to happen to Jerusalem will happen to the whole world. The destruction of Jerusalem prefigures the final end of the world. It is a sign of things to come.

The signs that we have already mentioned will precede historical events but are not signs of the end. "And when you hear of wars and rumors of wars, do not be alarmed," Jesus tells his four disciples; "this must take place, but *the end is not yet*" (Mk 13.7; Mt 24.6; Lk 21.9). "And then if any one says to you, 'Look, here is the Christ;' or 'Look, there he is!' *do not believe it*" (Mk 13.21; Mt 24.23). "The Gospel must first be preached to all nations" (Mk 13.10). Jesus saw that the Romans would destroy Jerusalem, and he predicted that great distress and wrath would fall upon the people: "They will fall by the edge of the sword, and be led captive among all nations; and Jerusalem will be trodden down by the Gentiles, until the times of the Gentiles are fulfilled" (Lk 21.24).

The Parousia, or the Second Coming, of the Son of Man, is not identical with the destruction of Jerusalem, but will come "after the tribulation." "The sun will be darkened, and the moon will not give its light, and the stars will be falling from heaven, and the powers in the heavens will be shaken. And then they will see the Son of Man coming in the clouds with great power and glory" (Mk 13.24–26; Mt 24.29–30; Lk 21.25–27). When will it happen? Is the end of the word imminent? These questions are answered in the recorded words of Christ. There are two sayings about the Last Judgment and Parousia at the end of his discourse, which must be given primary consideration. The first one runs as follows: "But of that day or that hour no one knows, not even the angels in heaven, nor the Son, but only the Father" (Mk 13.32). These words of Christ make all human calculations about the end utterly useless, in that they directly contradict Jesus' words. St Basil the Great also sees in this verse the Son's dependence upon the Father's will, as Jesus came and will come to fulfill the will of his Father. The second saying immediately follows the first one. Jesus said to the disciples, "Take heed, watch, for you do not know when the time will come" (Mk 13.33).

Whenever Jesus spoke about the end of the present age, of the Last Judgment, and of his Second Coming, he spoke with an

absolute certainty that these events would take place, and therefore he put stress upon readiness or watchfulness. The word
"watch" in Jesus' sayings and parables refers to the last days.
"*Watch* therefore—for you do not know when the master of the
house will come, in the evening, or at midnight, or at cockcrow,
or in the morning" (Mk 13.35). "And what I say to you I shall say
to all: '*Watch*'" (Mk 13.37). "That day" will come suddenly, therefore "*watch* at all times" (Lk 21.34). He speaks to them about the
days of Noah and compares them with the coming of the Son of
Man. Before the flood the people were enjoying themselves, eat-
ing, drinking, and marrying. They did this "until the day when
Noah entered the ark, and they did not know until the flood
came and swept them all away, so will be the coming of the Son
of Man . . . *Watch* therefore, you do not know on what day your
Lord is coming . . . for the Son of Man is coming at an hour you
do not expect" (Mt 24.37–44).

In the parables that refer to the Parousia, Jesus calls men to
watch. The early church understood the parable of the ten maidens in terms of Christ's Second Coming. Here the maidens, who
stand for the Christians, were expecting Christ (the bridegroom
of the parable). When they went out to meet him, he did not
come. Because his coming was delayed, some ceased to watch
and slept. Suddenly Christ appeared, and those who were not
ready for his coming were rejected (Mt 25.1–13).

This parable is followed by another one, the parable of the
talents (Mt 25.14–30), which again the early church interpreted
as a parable of the Second Coming. A man entrusted his prop-
erty to his servants. One of them received five talents, another

two, and a third one talent, "to each according to his ability."
How did the servants use these talents? The first one, who
received five, made five talents more. The second did likewise.
He traded with his two and succeeded in making two more. But
the third one did not use his talent but kept it hidden in a secure
place. The master came "after a long time" and settled accounts
with his servants. He praised the first two as faithful and said to
them: "You have been faithful over a little, I will set you over
much; enter into the joy of your master" (Mt 25.21,23). But the
third one was rebuked as a wicked and slothful servant, and was
rejected. The master "cast the worthless servant into outer darkness" (Mt 25.30). The opening word in this parable underlines
the importance of the last verse of the preceding one, which
ends: "Watch, therefore, for you know neither the day nor the
hour" (Mt 25.13). The parable of the talents begins, "*For* it will be
. . ." (Mt 25.14). It may be taken as a commentary on the meaning of the word "watch" or "watchfulness." This word does not
imply passivity or slothfulness, but activity and service.

Finally, this faithful service is defined in a concrete way in the
last parable, the parable of the Last Judgment (Mt 25.31–34).
Theo Preiss, in his work, *Life in Christ* (London: SCM Press,
Ltd, 1954), has translated and arranged this parable as follows so
as to emphasize its poetic qualities and its meaning:

> But when the Son of Man shall come in his glory
>   And the angels with him,
> Then shall he sit on the throne of his glory:
>   And before him shall be gathered all the nations:

And he shall separate them one from another,
As the shepherd separateth the sheep from the goats:
And he shall set the sheep on his right hand, but the
    goats, on his left.

Then shall the King say unto them on his right hand:
Come, ye blessed of my Father,
Inherit the kingdom prepared for you from the
    foundation of the world.
I was an hungered   and ye gave me meat:
I was thirsty   and ye gave me drink:
I was a stranger   and ye took me in:
I was naked   and ye clothed me:
I was sick   and ye visited me:
I was in prison   and ye came unto me.

Then shall the righteous answer him, saying:
Lord,
When saw we thee an hungered and fed thee?
Or, athirst, and gave thee drink?
And when saw we thee a stranger, and took thee in?
    or naked, and clothed thee?
And when saw we thee sick, or in prison, and came unto
    thee?

And the King shall answer and say unto them:
Verily I say unto you, Inasmuch as ye ministered unto one
of these my brethren, ye ministered unto me.

Then shall he say also unto them on the left hand:
Depart from me, ye cursed, into the eternal fire which is

prepared for the devil and his angels:
for I was an hungered   and ye gave me no meat:
I was thirsty   and ye gave me no drink:
I was a stranger   and ye took me not in:
    naked   and ye clothed me not:
    sick, and in prison   and ye visited me not.

Then shall they also answer saying:
    Lord, when saw we thee an hungered
        or athirst,
        or a stranger,
        or naked,
        or sick,
        or in prison,
    And did not minister unto thee?

Then shall he answer them, saying:
    Verily I say unto you,
        Inasmuch as ye did it not unto one of these
            least ye did it not unto me.
    And these shall go away into eternal punishment:
        But the righteous into eternal life.

The Son of Man in his Second Coming comes in the fullness of his Glory and appears before the whole world. He is the judge of "all the nations," and every man is judged according to his works (Rom 2.6). At the Last Judgment, the Son of Man identifies himself with the multitude of men who did the will of the Father. He lived in many, and many lived in him.

The parable of the Last Judgment takes us back to the teaching of Jesus, known as "the Sermon on the Mount" (Mt 5–7). The following beatitudes in particular are directly linked with this parable. "Blessed are the poor in spirit, for theirs is the kingdom of heaven" (Mt 5.3). "The poor in spirit" are those who voluntarily left everything in order to follow Christ. They prefer him to anything else. For them to follow him means to imitate Christ in their daily lives. "Blessed are the meek, for they shall inherit the earth" (Mt 5.5). Whereas the first proclaims what the true relation of the human being to God and his kingdom is, the second speaks about the spirit in which a person should deal with others. Therefore the meek are those who "empty" themselves of any personal prerogatives and, like the "poor in spirit," consider, approach, help, and work with others. This beatitude is followed by "Blessed are those who hunger and thirst for righteousness, for they shall be satisfied" (Mt 5.6). To hunger and thirst is to ask for something with one's whole being. Here it means to participate fully in a prayer that God's will shall be realized and fulfilled everywhere. It implies perfect dependence upon and obedience to God's will. It is also expressed in a petition in the Lord's Prayer, "Thy will be done, on earth as it is in heaven." And finally, one more beatitude is relevant for an understanding of the parable of the Last Judgment. "Blessed are the merciful, for they shall obtain mercy" (Mt 5.7). This beatitude describes yet another characteristic of one who is a follower, and not an admirer, of Christ. The merciful are those who show mercy to others, for they themselves experienced God's mercy. They forgive others, for God has forgiven them. They do not wait for others to apologize for wrongs they did to them, for God forgave them while they were still unrepentant sinners. The merciful love others, for God has poured his love into their hearts. "This is my commandment, that you love one another as I have loved you" (Jn 15.12).

The standards of judgment are those already proclaimed in the Son of Man's Sermon on the Mount. In other words, those who have practiced active love will inherit the kingdom. It is "the law of Christ." What about heathens, who never heard the gospel preached? They too will be judged, by whether or not they showed in their lives and in dealing with others the power of active love. St Paul writes that God judges the secrets of all by Christ, and "when Gentiles who have not the law do by nature what the law requires, they are a law to themselves, even though they do not have a law" (Rom 2.14).

It may seem as if the parable gives exclusive importance to giving alms, and thus minimizes the role of the church's faith and its doctrine. This impression would be quite wrong. Active love implies living faith. This faith is centered upon him, and each dogma tells us about him and guides us to him. "His coming before the world will simply attest the fact that all this time he has been present in men's souls and in the church" [E. Mersch, *The Whole Christ* (Milwaukee: The Bruce Publishing Company, 1938)]. At the end, he will identify himself with the members of his Body, as he did with his disciples whom Saul, the future apostle Paul, was persecuting. When Saul approached Damascus, "suddenly a light from heaven flashed about him," he fell to the ground, and heard a voice, "Saul, Saul, why do you persecute me?" Saul asked, "Who are you, Lord?" And the Lord answered,

"I am Jesus, whom you are persecuting" (Acts 9.1–5).

The parable of the Last Judgment ends Jesus' discourses in Jerusalem. It sums up what Jesus said and did there. In a way, the parable is the end of his farewell discourse. He is about to be lifted up from the earth and will die on the cross. Before this event takes place, he speaks of his identity with those who will be blessed and who will be given the gifts of meekness and mercy and obedience to God's will, and who will show them to others. They will receive the gift of salvation. In spite of all their works of love, God's salvation will not be given them on the basis of their merits, but again as a gift. When they have done all that is commanded them to do, they will say, "We are unworthy servants; we have only done what was our duty" (Lk 17.10). At this moment, just before his departure (*exodus*, death), Jesus makes identification. The Son of Man who stands before the people is the judge of the present age and the king of the age to come. This had been conveyed before, when he spoke after Peter's confession to the multitude, as well as to the disciples, about what it means to follow him. "If any man would come after me, let him deny himself and take up his cross and follow me" (Mk 8.34). That is, let him be poor in spirit, meek, and merciful. Let him hunger and thirst for righteousness. Let him lose his life "for my sake and the gospel's, and he will save it" (Mk 8.35). Then he added, "Whoever is ashamed of me and of my words in this adulterous and sinful generation, of him will the Son of Man also be ashamed, when he comes in the glory of his Father with the holy angels" (Mk 8.38). At the end of his teaching ministry in Jerusalem, Christ speaks openly about himself and his Second Coming.

III

The Night Before
the Crucifixion

O N WEDNESDAY, two days before the Passover, the chief
priests, the scribes, and the elders of the people gathered
in the palace of the high priest, Caiaphas, and once more dis-
cussed the problem of what to do about Jesus. This time their
main problem was "how to put him to death." They tried to avoid
killing him during the feast, for they feared the people and were
afraid that Jesus' removal would cause a tumult among them (Mt
26.1–15; Mk 14.1–2; Lk 22.1–2). They soon were forced to modify
their decision, however. On the same day that the religious representatives took counsel "to arrest Jesus by stealth and kill him,"
Judas, one of the Twelve, visited the chief priests and offered
them his service. When they heard Judas' offer, "they were glad"
(Mk 14.11; Lk 22.5). They needed Judas, for he would be able to
lead them to the place where Jesus would be spending the night.
If the arrest took place during the night, any possible conflict
with the multitude would be avoided. From the time of Judas'
visit, there was determination among the ruling council to
accomplish what they intended to do as soon as possible. They

could not miss the opportunity that Judas gave them. On the other hand, Jesus was determined not to give himself up into lawless hands before he accomplished the mission for which he had come to Jerusalem.

Judas' betrayal immediately followed Jesus' anointing at Bethany. When a woman poured ointment on Jesus' head, Judas heard Jesus say, "In pouring this ointment on my body she has done it to prepare me for burial" (Mt 26.12). St Mark and St John, who also give us accounts of the anointing at Bethany, testified that Jesus regarded the woman's act as anointing him for burial. Is there any connection between this event and Judas' betrayal? They are connected by St Matthew and St Mark. One interpretation is that Judas was looking for a political Messiah, and expected, in spite of the predictions of the Passion, that Jesus was going to perform this role. After Jesus connected the anointing with his burial, however, Judas' hopes were destroyed. Jesus was not what he expected him to be. Disappointed, he went to see Jesus' enemies. The Gospels do not say anything about Judas' destroyed expectation, and therefore we speculate about his motives. According to the evangelists, Judas' interest in "money" appeared to play the most significant role in his betrayal of Jesus. St Matthew recorded that first of all he asked for money, in return for betraying Jesus. St Mark, on the other hand, maintained that after Judas disclosed his plan he was promised money. In both accounts money takes a central place. At the time of Jesus' anointment, Judas Iscariot was the one who was indignant with the woman (Mary, the sister of Lazarus) for pouring costly ointment, according to St John, and who said, "Why was the ointment not sold for three hundred *denarii* and given to the poor?" (Jn 12.5). Then the evangelist adds, "This he said, not that he cared for the poor but because he was a thief, and as he had the money box he used to take what was put into it" (Jn 12.6).

The Gospel writers, however, go beyond "money" to indicate a further motive for Judas' betrayal. St Luke says that "Satan entered into Judas." Then "he went away and conferred with the chief priests and captains how he might betray him (Jesus) to them" (Lk 22.3–4). Even in St Luke, "money" is not left out. They were "engaged to give him money" (Lk 22.5). And in the Gospel according to St John, Christ pointed to Judas as a devil already in the early part of his ministry (Jn 6.70–71), and during the Last Supper St John records that "Satan entered into him." He left the room, "and it was night." What Judas loved above everything was "darkness." He "loved the darkness rather than light . . . every one who does evil hates the light, and does not come to the light, lest his deeds should be exposed" (Jn 3.19–21). Judas yielded to the first attack of the tempter. He was Satan's slave, for Satan entered into him. "Money," which Judas loved so much and preferred to anything else, is only an expression of the "darkness" that he voluntarily accepted and that ruled in him and over him. It was a concrete symbol of Judas' fall on the spiritual level. He was under no necessity to betray Jesus. He could have refused Satan, who had found his way into his heart. He had the choice of rejecting or accepting the opportunity. On the other hand, it was the will of God that the Son of Man *must* suffer, "but woe to that man by whom the Son of Man is betrayed! It would have been better for that man if he had not been born" (Mk 14.21).

The Last Supper

On Thursday Jesus took the initiative. His hour, the hour of salvation, was near. He sent Peter and John into the city: "Go and prepare the Passover for us, that we may eat it" (Lk 22.8). Christ is ready for what is about to happen.

The meal that Jesus had with his disciples was a Passover meal. Celebrating the Passover meant to celebrate the deliverance of Israel from Egypt, and to look with hope at the future, to a new divine deliverance. By this celebration, a Jew participates in the past and lives in future expectation.

While Jesus was sharing the same table with his disciples, he started to indicate that one of them would betray him. The disciples were sorrowful; they did not know whom he had in mind. In chapter 13 of the Gospel according to St John, Jesus is described as making a step-by-step disclosure of the identity of the traitor. After washing the disciples' feet, he said that all of them were not clean, referring to the one who would betray him. Then he quoted Psalm 41.9: "He who ate my bread has lifted his heel against me." Troubled in spirit, he spoke: "Truly, truly I say unto you, one of you will betray me." Still his disciples were ignorant about whom he was speaking. Therefore Peter asked John, the Beloved Disciple, who "was lying close to the breast of Jesus," to tell the others who it was that would betray his master. Then John said to Jesus, "Lord, who is it?" And Jesus disclosed the identity of the traitor by giving Judas a morsel.

Judas left the table before the institution of the Eucharist. The Lord's Supper was instituted at the end of the Passover meal, when Jesus spoke the words and performed the acts that transcended the celebration of the Passover. He took bread, blessed it, broke it and gave it to his disciples, saying, "This is my body, which is given for you. Do this in remembrance of me" (Lk 22.19, and parallels Mt 26.26; Mk 14.22). Then he took the cup, saying, "This cup which is poured out for you is the new covenant in my blood" (Lk 22.20, and parallels Mt 26.27–28; Mk 14.23–25). The phrase "which is poured out for you" means "which is poured out for many" (Mk 14.24; Mt 26.28), a Hebraic way of saying "which is poured out for all." While instituting the Eucharist, Jesus speaks about his approaching death. Here we have another reference by Christ himself to the Suffering Servant of God. Jesus' mission is the mission of the Servant. His death will be "for many" and it is precisely the all-embracing thought of Isaiah's prophecy. On that night before his death, the disciples participate already in the suffering of Christ, and before his Crucifixion he is present visibly and mystically. He is *with* his disciples, and now, by instituting the Eucharist, he is also *in* them. Christ's "mystical existence," stresses E. Mersch in his book, *The Whole Christ*, comes before the end of his "visible existence." Thus the identity and the continuity of the two is preserved. With his death and the pouring out of his blood, a new covenant, that is, a new and final relationship between God and man, will be inaugurated. By speaking about the covenant, Jesus points out that he will suffer death and that the new covenant will be sealed and dedicated with the blood of the beloved Son, as the old covenant was dedicated with the blood of sacrificed animals (Ex 24).

There is no precise record of the institution of the Eucharist in the Gospel according to St John. However, he knew about it. He did not omit the institution of the Lord's Supper through ignorance. The Evangelist John interwove it in the narrative in chapters 13–17 of his Gospel. The meaning of the Eucharist is given in Christ's discourse about the bread of life in chapter six. While he was still in Galilee and after feeding the five thousand, Jesus spoke about himself as the bread of Life. "I am bread which came down from heaven" (Jn 6.41).

> Truly, truly, I say unto you, unless you eat the flesh of the Son of man and drink his blood, you have no life in you; he who eats my flesh and drinks my blood has eternal life, and I will raise him up at the last day. For my flesh is food indeed, and my blood is drink indeed. He who eats my flesh and drinks my blood abides in me, and I in him. As the living Father sent me, and I live because of the Father, so he who eats me will live because of me (Jn 6.53–57).

The language used in this passage excludes any nonliteral or allegorical interpretation. The Greek text demonstrates even more clearly that it is intended to be interpreted literally; more so than can be ascertained from the translations. St John bears witness that the saying just quoted created difficulties for many of Jesus' disciples. "This is a hard saying; who can listen to it?" (Jn 6.60). Then Jesus, "knowing in himself that his disciples murmured at it," spoke to them about his Ascension and the activity of the Holy Spirit "that gives life," but many still did not understand. They "drew back and no longer went about with him" (Jn 6.66).

Another difference, this time a chronological discrepancy, that exists between the first three Gospels, on the one hand, and the fourth Gospel on the other, is related to the time when the Last Supper occurred. The first three Gospels are known as the Synoptic Gospels, meaning they may be viewed together, as they have a common order of events and subject matter. According to the Synoptic Gospels, it is the Passover meal and it happened on the Passover day. The Jews reckoned a day from sunset to sunset. Therefore the Last Supper, with the institution of the Eucharist and the Crucifixion, took place on the Passover day, on Friday (Thursday after sunset). St John is in full agreement with other evangelists that the Last Supper was held on Thursday evening and the Crucifixion on Friday. However, according to some references in the fourth Gospel, particularly Jn 19.31, the Passover fell on Saturday and not on Friday.

There is no generally accepted solution to this chronological difficulty. But it may be added that all four Gospels state the same thing theologically. In the life and death of Christ, the Passover is fulfilled and the new covenant is inaugurated. In St John's Gospel, Christ is the Lamb of God (Jn 1.29), who died at the time when paschal lambs were being selected and killed on the eve of the Passover. Perhaps St John synchronized these two events, Christ's death on the cross and the slaughtering of the paschal lambs, in order to convey that Christ is the true paschal lamb, "who takes away the sin of the world." Similarly, when St John put the cleansing of the temple at the beginning of Jesus' ministry, he did not do so in order to correct the accounts of the other three evangelists. He wanted, we think, to show that the life of Christ, the Word of God that became human, was from the very beginning a life of suffering.

The Passover that Jesus celebrated with his disciples was a memorial. The Lord's Supper is also a memorial day, but it is not done in remembrance of the miracle of Exodus but in remembrance of Christ. With the words "Do this in remembrance of me," writes St John Chrysostom, Jesus removes the disciples from the Jewish Passover, the paschal meal eaten in remembrance of the miracle in Egypt, and requires them to gather together in remembrance of him. The words "Do this" do not imply an option, but express a demand, a commandment without any qualifications.

In addition to its memorial significance, his Eucharist prefigured Jesus' sacrifice on the cross, his Resurrection and Ascension. "I tell you I shall not drink again of this fruit of the vine until that day when I drink it new with you in my Father's kingdom" (Mt 26.29).

The outcome of Christ's proclamation of the Gospel, the good news of salvation, and of his mission is the apostolic church. From the very beginning, the activity of the incarnate Son of God started with calls to individuals to follow him. He drew human beings to him. He saw Simon and Andrew and said to them, "Follow me," and they followed him. He called James and his brother John, and they left their father Zebedee in order to follow Jesus. He appointed the Twelve "to be with him." After Peter's confession, he promised that he would build his church. At the Last Supper he instituted the Eucharist, which is organically linked with the church and is indeed its life. The identity of the historical Jesus, who spoke these words, with the Resurrected and the Coming Christ is preserved in the sacrament of the Eucharist. In the parable of the vine, given in the context of the Last Supper, Christ spoke about this unity with those who abide in him:

> "Abide in me, and I in you. As the branch cannot bear fruit by itself unless it abides in the vine, neither can you, unless you abide in me. I am the vine, you are the branches. He who abides in me, and I in him, he it is that bears much fruit, for apart from me you can do nothing" (Jn 15.4–5).

This is the eucharistic unity, the unity of Christ with the members of his church.

Christ in Gethsemane

On the way to Gethsemane, after the institution of the Eucharist, Christ prophesied that all the disciples would fall away. When Peter objected and remarked that he would not, Jesus answered him, "Truly I say to you, this very night, before the cock crows twice, you will deny me three times." In Gethsemane he took Peter, James, and John, the three who saw his glory on the Mount of Transfiguration, to be witnesses of another glory, the glory of his obedience, manifested at the moment when he was facing death. He prayed, "Abba, Father, all things are possible to thee; remove this cup from me; yet not what I will but what thou wilt" (Mk 14.36; Mt 26.39; Lk 22.42). "Abba" is the Aramaic word that Jesus used for "Father." Only he used this expression. When he taught his disciples the Lord's Prayer, he asked them to pray "Our Father . . . ," but he himself never used the expression "our Father" when he addressed the Father, only "Abba," "the Father," or "my Father." The word was not used in Jewish prayers of the first century, and it expresses the most intimate and unique relationship between the Son and the Father. In Gethsemane the perfect obedience of the Son to the Father is once again manifested. It does not imply the subordination of the Son to the Father but indicates their unity, their oneness. "I and the Father are one" (Jn 10.30).

There is a direct connection between the Temptation of Christ, the Lord's Prayer, and his struggle in Gethsemane. Christ never taught anything that he himself did not first fulfill. In the Lord's Prayer, he asked the disciples to pray, "Thy will be done, on earth as it is in heaven." This he fulfilled in every work he performed, in every event of his life. The Lord's Prayer reflects his temptation in the wilderness. The petitions about daily bread, deliverance from temptations, and the evil one recall the three temptations in the wilderness. Again, in Gethsemane, Jesus fulfills the will of the Father and overcomes temptation. St Luke, who ends the story of the temptation of Christ with the words that the devil "departed from him until an opportune time" (Lk 4.13), connects the temptation in the wilderness with the suffering in the garden (Lk 22.39–46).

Christ, who voluntarily accepted suffering, prayed in Gethsemane, and his disciples, although told to watch and pray that they might not enter into temptation, slept (Mt 26.41; Mk 14.38; Lk 22.46). On the way to Gethsemane the disciples were ready to say that they preferred to die with him than to deny him (Mt 26.35; Mk 14.31), but nevertheless they could not watch and pray for a while, not for Jesus but for their own sakes. From this we learn, according to St John Chrysostom, "That a man's willingness is not sufficient, unless any one receive the help from above. And again we shall gain nothing by the help from above if there is not a willingness."

Christ before the Sanhedrin

While Jesus was still in the garden, talking with his disciples, Judas came with soldiers to arrest him. Judas "knew the place; for Jesus often met there with his disciples" (Jn 18.2), but the chief priests and the Pharisees did not. After Christ raised up Lazarus, they "had given orders that if any one knew where he was, he should let them know, so that they might arrest him" (Jn 11.57). Now Judas came with "a crowd with swords and clubs, from the chief priests and the scribes and the elders" (Mt 26.47; Mk 14.43). The Sanhedrin had its own police. Some of them had the duty of keeping order on the Temple grounds, and another special group was engaged, if the situation so demanded, to intervene outside the temple. The "crowd" that arrested him belonged to this Temple force. The arrest of Christ was done at night. It was planned in this way in order not to produce any commotion among the people, for the people saw in Jesus a man sent by God. Christ's words and works had made an impact upon them. Consequently, Judas' readiness to lead them to Gethsemane made Thursday night the most opportune time for the Sanhedrin to seize Jesus. Everybody was busy with the celebration of the Passover. There was little possibility of unrest among the people. The Sanhedrin was empowered by the Roman procurator legally to arrest a person. It is doubtful that the Roman soldiers took part. St John, in his account of the arrest, used two terms, "band" (*speira*) and "captain" (*chiliarchos*), which may point to the participation by the Romans in capturing Christ. There are two objections to this interpretation, however. First, the Jewish historian Josephus used both terms for Jewish military bodies and officers. Second, as soon as Jesus was arrested, he was immediately led to the high priests, and not to Pilate.

Christ was ready for Judas' coming. Nothing surprised him. He knew that the final act of the drama for the salvation of mankind was taking place. From Gethsemane he was led to Annas, a former high priest but still extremely powerful, who had executed the duties of high priest from AD 6 to AD 15. The Roman procurator whom Pilate succeeded had deposed him, but his influence upon the affairs of the Temple continued. Annas had five sons, and he managed somehow to make every one of them the high priest in the period between AD 16 and AD 44. Caiaphas, who was the high priest during Christ's ministry, death, and resurrection, was Annas' son-in-law. Therefore it is not surprising to read in St John's Gospel that Jesus, first of all, was led to Annas (Jn 18.12–14). The former high priest, who had lost the office but not the title, asked Jesus about his disciples and his teaching.

"I have spoken openly to the world," Jesus answered Annas; "I have always taught in synagogues and in the temple, where all Jews come together; I have said nothing secretly. Why do you ask me? Ask those who have heard me, what I said to them; they know what I said" (Jn 18.20–21). For such an answer to the high priest, Jesus was struck by an officer.

As soon as Jesus was brought to Caiaphas, the real trial began. Everybody was ready for it. The questioning of the witnesses started. "False witnesses came forward, but their witness did not agree" (Mt 26.60; Mk 14.56). According to Deuteronomy, "A single witness shall not prevail against a man for any crime or for any wrong in connection with any offence that he has committed; only on the evidence of two witnesses, or of three witnesses, shall a charge be sustained" (19.15). We are not told what they witnessed to, but we may imagine that Jesus' attitude toward the Law and the Sabbath was in the center of their testimony. "At last two came forward" and testified that Jesus had said, "I will destroy this temple that is made with hands, and in three days I will build another, not made with hands" (Mk 14.58 and Mt 26.61). St John records this saying about the destruction of the Temple after the cleansing of the Temple, but in a different way and with different emphasis: "Destroy this temple and in three days I will raise it up" (Jn 2.19). After the Resurrection his disciples understood that he then "spoke of the temple of his body" (Jn 2.21).

Jesus did not defend himself. He kept silent. The testimony of the last two witnesses did not agree. The trial, however, did not end. Caiaphas, with all his authority as high priest, interfered with the proceedings and asked Jesus, "Are you the Christ, the Son of the Blessed?" (Mk 14.61 and parallels Mt 26.63 and Lk 22.67). Jesus, who had kept silent when he was falsely accused, now spoke when he had to proclaim who he was: "I am; and you will see the Son of Man sitting at the right hand of power, and coming with the clouds of heaven" (Mk 14.62, and parallels Mt 26.64; Lk 22.69–70). Caiaphas asked, "Are you the Christ, the Son of God?" and Jesus answered affirmatively. The word "the Blessed" and in Jesus' answer, the word "power" are roundabout expressions for God. For the Jews, the Messiah was to be a human being and was inferior to God. That God has a Son and that Jesus claimed to be this Son of God, for Caiaphas, was "ultimate impiety."

But above all Jesus had said, "I am," or "I am he." This expression, used by Jesus in answering Caiaphas' question, is to be found in several places in the fourth Gospel. "I am" is a divine formula. At one point in his ministry it was recorded by St John in 8.58–59 that when Jesus applied this expression to himself he was in danger of being stoned. Commenting on Jesus' saying before the Sanhedrin, E. Stauffer writes in *Jesus and His Story* (New York: Alfred A. Knopf, 1959) that the expression "I am" "... was the purest, the boldest, and the profoundest declaration of Jesus of who and what he was ... It was the boldest declaration. 'I am he'—this meant: where I am, there God is, there God lives and speaks, calls, asks, acts, decides, loves, chooses, forgives, rejects, suffers, and dies ... The historical epiphany [manifestation] of God was fulfilled in the form of a man ... God himself had become man ..." Jesus' answer to the high priest's question was a revelation of the mystery of his person. Caiaphas understood what was expressed and meant by Jesus' answer. Therefore he "tore his mantle and said, 'Why do we still need witnesses?'"

(Mk 14.63, Mt 26.65). By tearing his mantle in a symbolic way, he expressed that Jesus was guilty of blasphemy. "You have heard his blasphemy," Caiaphas added. To the high priest's question, "What is your judgment?" the members of the Sanhedrin answered, "He deserves death" (Mt 26.66 and Mk 14.64).

After being sentenced to death he was exposed to further humiliation, being spat on and struck. Then followed Peter's denial. At the time of his arrest all the disciples forsook him and fled (Mt 26.56, Mk 14.50). But when Jesus was led to the high priest, Peter appeared and followed his master "at a distance, right into the courtyard of the high priest" (Mk 14.54, and parallels Mt 26.58, Lk 22.54). When maids and bystanders asked him about his connection with the arrested and accused Jesus, Peter denied three times that he knew the man. Then he remembered with words of Jesus, "'Before the cock crows twice you will deny me three times.' And he broke down and wept" (Mt 26.75, Mk 14.72, Mk 22.61–62).

IV

The Trial Before Pilate and the Crucifixion

THE SANHEDRIN sentenced Jesus to death for blasphemy. "He who blasphemes the name of the Lord shall be put to death; all the congregation shall stone him; the sojourner as well as the native, when he blasphemes the Name, shall be put to death" (Lev 24.16). A death sentence at the time of Jesus' trial could not be executed by the Sanhedrin. It had lost this power around AD 30. It retained the right to pass a death sentence, but a Jew sentenced to death must be handed over to the Roman authority for trial, where the previous sentence must be confirmed and then carried out by the Romans.

Political Trial

Jesus was delivered to Pilate on Friday morning. On that day those who brought Jesus before the governor produced charges against him. The charge of blasphemy was not mentioned at all, for they feared that the Roman governor would not act decisively upon this charge. Thus their charges against Jesus were now of a political nature. The Sanhedrin's strategy was based upon the consideration that Jesus must be accused of a crime punishable by death under Roman law. Therefore they said to Pilate that they found Jesus "perverting our nation"; then, as the second charge, they told the governor that Jesus was "forbidding us to give tribute to Caesar," and as the third, that he himself claimed to be "Christ, a king" (Lk 23.2). In their own trial, the Sanhedrin had condemned Jesus just because he was not the Messiah of their national expectation. "They now wanted to have him condemned by the pagan court on the allegation that he made claims corresponding precisely to their nationalistic messianic ideal," writes J. Blinzler in *The Trial of Jesus* (Westminster, MD: Newman Press, 1959). All three charges were purely political. The third one was the most dangerous. For Pilate it meant that this man Jesus was stirring the people up in order to restore the kingdom of Israel, that is, the Jewish national kingdom, and to expel the Romans from Palestine. In all four Gospels it is recorded that Pilate asked Jesus, "Are you the king of the Jews?" (Mt 27.11; Mk 15.2; Lk 23.3; as well as Jn 18.33). According to the first three Gospel writers, Jesus answered, "You have said so." In other words, you have said so, not I. And St John records Jesus' answer as follows: "Do you say this of your own accord, or did others say it to you about me?" (Jn 18.34). He then disclosed the nature of his messiahship to Pilate: "My kingdom is not of this world." His kingdom, with all its power and the authority that is related to it, has its source not in this world, but it comes from above. In other words, Christ's kingdom and Christ's authority are not of human but of divine origin. His activity or mission, however, extends to this whole world. "For God sent the Son into the world, not to condemn the world, but that the world might be saved through him" (Jn 3.17). When Pilate remarked, "So you are king?" Jesus pointed out what was involved in his kingship. He is not a king in Pilate's sense of the word, an agitator, a rebel king. He is the king who came into the world "to bear witness to the truth" (Jn 18.37–38). When Pilate asked him, "What is truth?" Jesus made no answer. Pilate misunderstood both the nature of his kingdom and the nature of his kingship. His misinterpretation of Jesus' words is manifested in his two questions: "So you are king?" and "What is truth?"

The chief priests and elders were pressing with their charges against Jesus. His only answer was his silence. The most dominant feature of the Passion narrative is precisely this silence of Christ. Pilate noticed something unusual about this man. Jesus did not intend to defend himself. From his own previous experience in dealing with other accused, the governor expected that Jesus would let loose a torrent of words in his own defense. Jesus, however, was silent, made no further answer, "not even to a single charge; so that the governor wondered greatly" (Mt 27.14, and parallel, Mk 15.5). And Pilate announced, "I find no crime in this man" (Lk 23.4). But the chief priest repeated the first charge, and the governor, to get ride of this case, and being told that Jesus was a Galilean, sent Jesus to Herod Antipas (Lk 23.6–16).

This Herod was the youngest son of Herod the Great, known to us from Matthew's Gospel, the one who had killed all the male children in Bethlehem (Mt 2). His son, Herod Antipas, ruled in Galilee, and he was responsible for the death of St John the Baptist. He had come to Jerusalem for the Passover.

In a few verses, St Luke describes this extraordinary confrontation between a king of this world and the king whose kingdom is not of this world, between Herod Antipas and Jesus. The
ruler of Galilee expected Jesus to make "some signs," some wonders. "He questioned him at some length," but Jesus "made no
answer." He was silent. Then Herod decided to treat Jesus "with
contempt," and, together with his soldiers, he "mocked him" and
sent him back to Pilate. The silence of Jesus recalls again the Suffering Servant of Isaiah 53, who was despised, bruised, and
oppressed; "yet he opened not his mouth" (Is 53.7). Here, as well
as before Pilate and the Sanhedrin, his silence judges those who
think that they judge him. Jesus does not defend himself when
falsely accused.

For Pilate, Jesus was innocent. He clearly perceived "that it
was out of envy that the chief priests had delivered him up" (Mk
15.10, and Mt 27.18). He hoped to save Jesus from the wrath of
the chief priests. On that Friday morning, Pilate reminded the
crowd: "You have a custom that I should release one man for you
at the Passover; will you have me release for you the king of the
Jews?" To his surprise, the multitude cried out, "Not this man,
but Barabbas" (Jn 18.39–40; Mk 15.9–11; and parallels). Pilate
scourged Jesus, his soldiers "plaited a crown of thorns," mocked
and struck him, all in hope that the masses would be satisfied
with this type of punishment. The answer was, "Crucify him!"
(Mk 15.14 and parallels). Then again Pilate stated that he found
no crime in Jesus. At this point the religious leaders introduced
the "religious charge" against Jesus. "We have a law, and by that
law he ought to die, because he has made himself the Son of

God" (Jn 19.7). The law to which they referred is Leviticus 24.16. Having heard this new charge, Pilate was afraid and wanted to release Jesus. But at the end of these proceedings, a threat was used as the final weapon to force Pilate to act: "If you release this man, you are not Caesar's friend; everyone who makes himself a king sets himself against Caesar." Immediately Pilate brought Jesus out and "sat down on the judgment seat" (Jn 19.13). This expression conveys that Pilate pronounced a formal, legal sentence, and it was the death sentence, for he delivered Jesus to be crucified.

The Responsibility for Christ's Death

Instead of asking for the release of Christ, the people shouted, "Release to us Barabbas!" Who was the man called Barabbas, whom the people preferred to Jesus? St Matthew characterized him as "a notorious prisoner"; St Mark as a rebel "who had committed murder in the insurrection"; St Luke described him in the same terms; and for St John, "Barabbas was a robber" (Mt 27.16; Mk 15.7; Lk 23.19; Jn 18.40). From all these sources, the portrait of Barabbas is clear and adequate. All that the evangelists say about him indicates that Barabbas was involved in the contemporary political movement and in action that was directed against the Romans. He was guilty of the very thing that Jesus was accused of by the members of the Sanhedrin before Pilate. The Barabbas case is an eloquent expression of the falsehood and utter insincerity of the chief priests and their helpers in the Sanhedrin.

We may assume that Barabbas was known to many as a national hero. It is quite possible that he had many followers among those who asked for his release and for the crucifixion of Jesus. The followers and disciples of Jesus were afraid, and, as we have seen, the Twelve had fled away. Barabbas' popularity was not enough to explain the change of heart in the people, however. Throughout the Passion Week, the people, the crowds or the multitudes, were with Jesus. This fact is well attested in the Gospel narrative. For this reason, the religious leaders were irritated, uneasy, and afraid. Their main task was to separate the people from Jesus. They arrested him at night, and they held his trial during the night, so that early in the morning they might announce that Jesus was a blasphemer and that according to the Law he ought to die. They had to convince the crowd that he was going to abolish the Law of God, the very foundation of their religion and their piety; that he spoke about himself in terms that were utterly irreligious; and that he proclaimed a new revelation. They acted as if what God had revealed in the past was good enough for them. Although the ruling body did not have the right to execute the death sentence, a trial probably was necessary if they wanted to change the people's attitude toward Jesus. The people's piety and their devotion to the Law were skillfully used for the realization of the aims of the religious leaders. The chief priests and elders, according to the Gospel accounts, "persuaded the people to ask for Barabbas and destroy Jesus" (Mt 27.20). They "stirred up the crowd" to have Pilate release Barabbas instead of Jesus (Mk 15.11). The history of the Passion is good source material for a study of the psychology of the masses. In the crowd it is only one step from an attitude of admiration to one of hostility.

What about Pilate and his attitude? The Roman governor did not have the moral strength to stay by his convictions and to suffer the consequences that might follow from this stand. Under the threat of the accusation that he was not Caesar's friend, he ceased all his efforts to release Christ. He was afraid of what might happen if some members of the Sanhedrin went to Rome and accused him there. The people had to choose between Jesus and Barabbas, and Pilate too had a choice: between Jesus and the Emperor Tiberius. To preserve himself and to save his position, he decided not to make the emperor suspicious about his dealing in Palestine, and he pronounced the death sentence on Jesus. His security meant more to him than a possible miscarriage of justice. Fundamentally, Pilate cared for and was sensitive to political power, and not to truth and justice.

Thus the sinless Jesus, "the Lamb of God," underwent two trials and all the sufferings connected with them and was found guilty of "religious" and "political" crimes. Both the Jews and the Gentiles took part in condemning him to death.

The Words from the Cross

The crucifixion was the Roman method of carrying out a death sentence. Cicero described it as "the most cruel and frightful sentence." To maintain peace and order in their occupied territories, the Romans used the crucifixion particularly for those who opposed their political power, as well as for slaves who had for various reasons left their masters' houses. Jesus, sentenced to death, was to carry his own cross. Later, Simon of Cyrene was

seized and ordered to carry it behind Jesus. On this journey to
Golgotha, a round hill, "a great multitude of the people" followed
him. And many women "bewailed and lamented him" (Lk
23.26–27). It was an expression of genuine sorrow. Jesus spoke to
them about the coming historical catastrophe, the destruction of
Jerusalem. "Daughters of Jerusalem, do not weep for me, but
weep for yourselves and for your children" (Lk 23.28). Two criminals who were to be put to death with Jesus were in this proces-
sion. When they reached Golgotha, Jesus was offered "wine
mingled with myrrh," but he refused to take it (Mk 15.23; Mt
27.33: "when he tasted it, he would not drink it"). It was the custom to give this drink to a condemned man in order to make him
less sensitive to pain, for crucifixion caused unbearable pain and
suffering. Jesus refused the drink and thus passed through all the
suffering while fully conscious.

An inscription was put above his cross: "This is the king of
the Jews." It had a double meaning. First, in accordance with
Pilate's intention, it pointed to the reason for which he was condemned. Secondly, it conveyed his claim that he was *the* king of
Israel. With regard to this inscription, there was a dispute
between Pilate and the chief priests. The latter suggested that
over Jesus' head the charge should be: "This man said, 'I am king
of the Jews'" (Jn 19.21). Pilate had yielded so much under pres-
sure and threats that he decided to assert his authority on this
minor point.

Christ was crucified at the third hour (nine a.m.). He was fas-
tened to his cross with nails. Another method was to fasten a
man to the cross with cords. That nails were used with Christ is

implied in the Gospel according to St John. When he appeared for the first time to his disciples after the resurrection, Thomas was not with them. The other disciples told him, "We have seen the Lord," but Thomas remarked, "Unless I see in his hands the print of the nails, and place my finger in the mark of the nails, and place my hand in his side, I will not believe" (Jn 20.24–25). Eight days after the first post-resurrection appearance, Jesus came again and stood among the disciples. This time Thomas was present. When Jesus told him: "Put your finger here . . ." Thomas answered, "My Lord and my God" (Jn 20.26–28).

From the cross Jesus spoke, and seven of his sayings were recorded in the Gospels. It is difficult to arrange them in a sequence, but we may assume that the first two from the Gospel according to St Luke were spoken by Christ before the others.

The first words of Christ from the cross were the words of the prayer of forgiveness: *"Father, forgive them; for they know not what they do"* (Lk 23.34). He was praying for *all* those who were responsible for his crucifixion, for the members of the San-hedrin, for the misled crowd that asked for his death, and for Pilate and his soldiers. While he was hanging on the cross, the mocking continued. The chief priests and scribes in a mocking way asked for a sign. "He saved others; he cannot save himself. Let the Christ, the king of Israel, come down from the cross, that we may see and believe" (Mk 15.31–32, and parallels). The soldiers mocked him also.

One of the criminals crucified with him reviled Jesus, whereas the other thief accepted his guilt and rebuked the first, for he saw in Jesus an innocent man. He asked to be remembered by Jesus when he came in his kingly power. To him Christ said, *"Truly, I say to you, today you will be with me in Paradise"* (Lk 23.43). Once again he reveals the mystery of his person: he who hung upon the cross, who suffered and who said *"I thirst"* (Jn 19.28), was the master of life and death. He promised to the criminal that he would enter into the life of blessedness on that very day.

Women who followed him from Galilee to Jerusalem were looking on from afar, and a few of them were standing by the cross. Among them was his mother, Mary. When he noticed his mother and his beloved disciple standing near, he committed them to each other. To his Mother he said, *"Woman, behold your son!"* and to the disciple, *"Behold your mother"* (Jn 19.26–27). The beloved disciple remained faithful. He became a pattern for every faithful follower of Christ. Mary, by becoming his mother, would become the mother of all followers of Christ, "the mother of all the faithful."

Then, about the ninth hour (three p.m.), "Jesus cried with a loud voice, *'Eloi, Eloi, lama sabachthani?'* which means, *'My God, my God' why hast thou forsaken me?'"* (Mk 15.34; Mt 27.46). This saying is a quotation of the first verse from Psalm 22. Jesus probably was reciting the psalm in its entirety. The psalmist goes on to say that he is "scorned by men and despised by the people (22.6). He is near death, and those around him started to divide his garments.

> A company of evildoers encircles me;
>   they have pierced my hand and feet—

I can count all my bones—
    they stare and gloat over me;
they divide my garments among them
    and for my raiment they cast lots.

                    (Ps 22.16–18)

These verses were fulfilled at the time of Jesus' crucifixion. "They divided his garments among them, casting lots for them, to decide what each should take" (Mk 15.24; Mt 27.35).

Then the sufferer, with full confidence, continues:

I will tell of your name to my brethren;
    in the midst of the congregation I will praise you:
You who fear the Lord, praise him!
For he has not despised or abhorred
    the affliction of the afflicted;
and he has not hid his face from him,
    but has heard, when he cried to him.
From you comes my praise in the great congregation;
    my vows I will pay before those who fear him.
The afflicted shall eat and be satisfied;
    those who seek him shall praise the Lord!
May your hearts live forever.

                    (Ps 22.22–26)

Psalm 22 is the prayer of a righteous suffered who is not alienated from God, but who loves, trusts, and has faith in him. Seen in the context of the psalm, the words, "My God, My God, why has thou forsaken me?" are not a cry of despair and do not mean that Jesus was forsaken by God. Due to Adam's transgression, say the Fathers of the Church, we were forsaken. Christ came to save the fallen, and through his perfect obedience and suffering on the cross we are accepted by God again. By this saying on the cross, Jesus represents us in his person, our abandonment and our reconciliation with God.

Before his death, Jesus said with a loud voice, *"Father, into thy hands I commit my spirit"* (Lk 23.46). With complete trust and in union with the Father, he died a voluntary death ("I commit my spirit"). Just before he yielded up his spirit, he said, *"It is finished"* (Jn 19.30), meaning, "It has been completed" or "it is consummated." The mission for which he had come was now accomplished at the moment of his death on the cross. His glory at this moment was revealed.

"I glorified you on earth, having accomplished the work which you gave me to do; and now, Father, glorify me in your own presence with the glory which I had with you before the world was made" (Jn 17.4–5).

When he died, "the curtain of the temple was torn in two, from top to bottom" (Mt 27.51; Mk 15.38). The curtain that separated the Holy Place from the Holy of Holies was removed. In the Holy place daily sacrifices were offered. The Holy of Holies was the place of God's invisible presence, and only the high priest could enter once a year. Thus the barrier that divided humanity from God disappeared. By Christ's death the separation between the two was overcome. The new relation between them was inaugurated. "He has broken down the dividing wall of hostility," writes St Paul, ". . . that he might reconcile us both to God in one body through the Cross, thereby bringing the hostility to an end" (Eph 2.14f).

The Roman soldier who took part in mocking, spitting, and striking Jesus (Mt 27.27–31; Mk 15.16–20) and finally with others led him away to the place of crucifixion was struck by the manner of Christ's death. When the centurion heard Jesus utter "a loud cry," and heard him saying, "Father, into thy hands I commit my spirit," he praised God and said, "Certainly this man was innocent" (Lk 23.47). "Truly this man was a son of God" (Mt 27.54; Mk 15.39).

The Scriptures were fulfilled, the mission completed, at the very moment when he "breathed his last." St John of Damascus wrote, "every action of Christ and all his working of miracles were truly very great and divine and wonderful, but of all things the most wonderful is his honorable cross." For by the Cross, he continues, all things are set aright. Sin is destroyed, death is overcome, and resurrection is bestowed. What Christ accomplished with death on the cross is made manifest in his Resurrection.

Conclusion

THE PASSION narrative in the Gospels is a calm, solemn presentation of historical events. More than any other part of the Gospel, this narrative has the most definite shape and historical detail. It is most explicit about Jesus' mission and its fulfillment. These dramatic events were from the very beginning proclaimed publicly, and believers and unbelievers alike were acquainted with them. If they had been historically unfounded, opponents of the early Christians would have had no trouble refuting them. Christ's crucifixion and trial are attested by the Jewish historian, Flavius Josephus (c. 37–97) in his book, *The Antiquities of the Jews*: "Although Pilate, following on denunciation by the leading men among us, punished him with the death of the cross, those who had loved him from the beginning did not cease from doing so."

The record of the Passion is neither anti-Jewish nor anti-Semitic, although it was later misused for this purpose. The account of the Passion was preserved and proclaimed first of all by the Christian community in Jerusalem, which was composed of Jewish Christians. The apostles, Jews by birth, used the story to convince Jews that Jesus is the Christ foretold in the Scriptures. A careful reading of the Passion narrative shows that there is no confusion between the responsibility of the leaders and that

of the people as a whole. Opposing "collective guilt," the prophet
Ezekiel had emphasized personal responsibility: "The son shall
not suffer for the iniquity of the father, nor the father suffer for
the iniquity of the son; the righteousness of the righteous shall
be upon himself, and the wickedness of the wicked shall be upon
himself" (Ezek 18.20).

The Passion narrative has been a problem and a puzzle for
many. Certain early Christian copyists, for example, found it difficult to accept that Jesus could pray even for those who were most
directly responsible for his death. When they came to the words,
"Father, forgive them, for they know not what they do," they simply omitted them. Another problem confronts modern Jewish
commentators. There is a tendency among them to try to vindicate the religious leaders of Jesus' time, and in this apologetic
effort they overlook historical facts. Any distortions such as these
obscure the real issue and even create more misunderstanding.

The Passion narrative can only be understood if we take into
account the Gospels as a whole, and, in an even larger context,
the Old Testament. Christ's Passion is the center of the Scripture, in that it throws light on all that has gone before, as well as
on all that has followed after. This center is an historical event,
the life, death, and resurrection of Christ. Christ deliberately
connected his ministry with the Old Testament in order that we
may grasp its full meaning. He was fully conscious of his role as
the Messiah, and he disclosed it to the people particularly during the Passion Week.

Bibliographical Note

Any reader who is interested in going into this subject in more detail may refer to the following works:

Blinzer, Josef. *The Trial of Jesus*. Westminster, MD: Newman Press, 1959.

Jeremias, Joachim. *The Central Message of the New Testament*. New York: Charles Scribner's Sons, 1965.

Kassian, Bishop. *Khristos i pervoye khristianskoy pokolenie* (Christ and the First Christian Generation, in Russian). Paris: YMCA, 1950.